HYDROPONICS FOR HOUSEPLANTS

Dedicated to Jean, who keeps track of it all!

And thanks to my editor, Kristin Kulsavage, for her excellent help along the way.

HYDROPONICS FOR HOUSEPLANTS

AN INDOOR GARDENER'S GUIDE TO GROWING WITHOUT SOIL

PETER LOEWER

Skyhorse Publishing

Skyhorse Publishing books may be purchased in bulk at special discounts for sales promotion, corporate gifts, fund-raising, or educational purposes. Special editions can also be created to specifications. For details, contact the Special Sales Department, Skyhorse Publishing, 307 West 36th Street, 11th Floor, New York, NY 10018 or info@skyhorsepublishing.com.

Skyhorse® and Skyhorse Publishing® are registered trademarks of Skyhorse Publishing, Inc.®, a Delaware corporation.

Visit our website at www.skyhorsepublishing.com.

10 9 8 7 6 5 4 3 2 1

Library of Congress Cataloging-in-Publication Data is available on file.

Cover design by Qualcom Designs
Cover photo credit: Peter Loewer

Print ISBN: 978-1-63450-492-8
Ebook ISBN: 978-1-5107-0165-6

Printed in the United States of America

Table of Contents

Preface

Initially, this book got its start many years ago when my wife and I came from the green fields of a rural community in upstate New York to rediscover all the bling and glitter that a big city has to offer. We settled in the Lower East Side of Manhattan, four flights up, into a small floor-through apartment with two windows facing an airshaft and two front windows facing the street. Our front door was made of some legendary wood with a frosted-glass window reinforced with chicken wire, and there was not a piece of clover in sight.

After the first three months of a typical New York winter, we needed something to remind us of our country heritage and decided to buy a few house plants to brighten our home environment. Since variety stores in our neighborhood were few and far between, we visited a local florist and bought a Christmas pepper (*Capsicum annuum*), the florist having told us that "Nothing on God's green earth can kill them!", a mother-in-law's tongue (*Sansevieria trifasciata*)—also called a snake plant, a rather limp philodendron of unknown parentage, and an African violet (*Saintpaulia ionantha*).

Like most newly-arrived New Yorkers, we spent most of our free time away from the apartment, and the steam heat began to have its effect: the violet leaves turned brown and crinkled up, despite endless soakings in the sink. In fact, one evening, in darkness (the bathroom light was inoperable; it was behind the door, which had to be left open to admit heat from the kitchen as the landlord had completely overlooked any source of warmth for the bathroom) I neglected to notice that Jean had placed the plants in the tub for a needed soak. One blast from the shower, and a great deal of soil went down the drain and up the walls.

After cleaning up, we went foraging for soil from Central Park and filled a small brown paper bag with needed dirt, which we smuggled home on the subway.

Upon repotting with what turned out to be real (and tainted) soil, some insects—including white flies—arose from their winter slumber and tore the pepper to shreds.

Then, in late March, the heat inside the apartment soared to 95° with the windows and the hall door open. The plants were parched. Because the cold-water pipes had broken that afternoon and no one in the building had cold water, we put pans of hot water in the refrigerator to cool, but to no avail—the plants expired.

Upon moving to our next apartment, I remembered my mother's garden and her endless plant cuttings, quietly rooting in old jelly glasses filled with water on the kitchen window sill and enclosed back porch. Why not just grow our plants in water? There would be no pots, no dirt, and no daily watering. We wouldn't have to transform the bathroom or kitchen into a potting shed.

We started with some ivy cuttings donated by a Long Island friend, and from then on, at first in the city, then more recently in our Asheville home, our water garden has been growing and growing.

1

Why Water?

Hydroponics, or hydroculture (growing plants in water), has a history of over 300 years, from the first experiments by the English botanist John Woodward (who endeavored to discover how plants received their nutrients from soil) on to the giant glass and plastic, fully automated, factory greenhouses of the twenty-first century, where vegetables from watercress to tomatoes are grown commercially by the ton.

On a more homely scale, the Sunday supplements of the late 1930s had many readers believing that a small tank near the kitchen would soon produce all the vegetables, fruits, and salads needed by a healthy, modern family.

By the 1940s, popular magazines and newspapers predicted that whole armies would be fed by plants grown without soil in food factories that operated twenty-four hours a day, using giant sunlamps to replace the sun. Visions of super squashes danced in the heads of farmers (released from toil in the fields) and vegetable buyers in box stores alike.

Even today, hydroponic speculations conjure up elaborate spaceship gardens that utilize the wastes of the crew for the necessary carbon dioxide and nutrients to produce extra-terrestrial fruits and juicy algae.

For earth-bound gardeners, the promise of hydroponics is more modest—and much closer at hand. The satisfactions of water gardening are available to anyone who likes a bit of greenery in the home all year round and who will spare five minutes a week for the care of their plants. No doubt any reader who picks up this book has tried his or her hand with houseplants. No doubt you have had some success, but those successes, unless you have an uncommonly green thumb, have been mixed with frequent failures. And I'll wager that most of your failures can be traced to one single problem: improper watering!

Before I took up hydroponics, I found I invariably missed one of my house plants on my watering rounds. I thought I had everything down to a perfect schedule: plant X gets water once a week only in the summer (except on rainy days) and in the winter when the leaves begin to droop, plant Y gets water twice a day, and plant Z gets water on the first day of spring. Suddenly, I'd have to go away for a few days and return to find not only X, but Y and Z as well, in small heaps on desiccated soil.

With water gardening, I just make sure all the vessels are full before leaving and return in a week, or even two, to find all leaves lush and green.

∧ An attractive centerpiece made from an old glass battery jar, clear glass marbles, and rooted cuttings of an umbrella plant, Chinese evergreen, ribbon plant, gold-dust *Dracaena*, and a wandering inch plant.

Not only does the practice of hydroponics substantially increase your success as an indoor gardener, it also makes you a wizard decorator as well. The decorative possibilities of the plants and their root systems forming fantastic patterns in the glassware are endless. If you need a unique centerpiece for a dinner party, while setting the table, just go to your water garden and remove two or three plants of pleasing colors and textures, wash them roots and all, then combine them in an attractive jar or vase, add a few glass marbles or pebbles for support—and water—and you have it made—without a costly trip to the florist.

Hydroponics is already a busy and booming hobby, so special pots and vessels are available on the Internet. Most ware is based on the plants growing in special water-absorbent granules in an inner perforated pot placed within an outer plastic waterproof container or reservoir pot—some utilitarian and some with a decorating splash. Nutrients are provided by adding liquid fertilizer to the water reservoir at the bottom of the container.

I actually have and use a French self-watering pot made of black plastic called a Riviera Cube 10. It sported a small wick to pull up water from a bottom reservoir, was made and developed in France some fifty years ago—and is still being used.

However, even with the web, there are many areas where such information is not available, and commercial equipment is missing, too. So we'll launch you on a water-gardening career that is relatively inexpensive (no mean feat, that), generally carefree, and as creative and involved as you wish to make it. Furthermore, we can guarantee that you will have no soil-borne pests and diseases, and no problems of what to do with that half-bushel of dank soil that always spills on the floor halfway to the garbage bin.

∧ A commercial U.S. hydroculture pot with a plant being grown in a nutrient solution.

Unfortunately, using my methods you will not be able to grow a crop of ten-pound zucchinis and heaps of lush red tomatoes (you have to consult the world of vegetable hydroponics for such directions). But I can certainly help you fill that empty counter in front of the living room window with a picture of variegated green that will be a delight for months, even years to come. ...

2

Getting Started

I've always hated books with page upon page of rules. And I've mentioned before that water gardening is simple, so I shall not dwell on instructions of things to do and just start with a quick list of things you will need for your garden and a few basic tricks of the trade.

CONTAINERS

Use any vessel that will hold water—except for copper, brass, or lead containers, which generate harmful chemicals as they interact with water and with plant food.

There is an entire chapter on finding and making containers toward the end of the book (see page 81); here, allow me to ruminate about clear glass versus colored glass. The main objection to clear glass in hydroponics is that, with a strong light source and extra nutrients, a large quantity of algae will soon show up. The darker the glass, the fewer algae plants will appear. Algae (the singular word is alga) are simple nonflowering plants in a large group that includes a number of seaweeds and many single-celled varieties. Like all plants, the algae contain chlorophyll but lack true stems, roots, vascular tissues, and leaves. They can be very unattractive as residents in your plant's water; in an opaque container, there will be no algae at all.

Despite this discussion, I'm a clear-glass advocate myself. Because I've never had more than ten or twenty containers in use at one time and, as replacement materials are, to say the least, inexpensive, I find the routine of changing waters, rinsing the roots, and reshaping my plants, about once a month or so, a very relaxing way to spend an evening.

The best argument for clear glass is that I find the root development of my water plants just as fascinating as the growth of greenery on top. Some authorities claim that sunlight damages roots, but I don't believe it (unless they are left totally unprotected in a hot summer sun so that the water virtually boils them to death). In the end, the choice of glassware is entirely up to you.

STONES AND GRAVELS

In the right containers, many plants need no support other than the sides of the vessel itself. Many other plants may need support at first, but soon their roots will fill the container bottom and provide a firm base.

When my water-grown plants need support, or a "holdfast," I've always used aquarium gravel purchased at a local pet shop. Beach pebbles are grand-looking, but make sure they are absolutely clean of sea salt, even if you found them well beyond the high-tide line. Beach sand, while sparkly and attractive, is too heavily laced with salt ever to be sufficiently rinsed clean in the kitchen sink. Marble chips eventually change the acid/alkaline balance of the water, so I've been told, so their use is, or would be, an experiment. Bricks, broken into small pieces, are usable. Clear glass marbles make beautiful holdfasts; being a purist at heart, I dislike the colored varieties.

Finally, there are a few plants that like to have their roots surrounded by some kind of soil—some of the pitcher plants come to mind—so I found that ground up rocks (usually black and the size of sand granules) found at the local hobby store were perfect for that use.

And if you check into many of the supplies available to gardeners who graduate into advanced hydroculture, you will find mention of another growing medium called expanded clay pellets. These are inert pellets that are described as being pH neutral, basically inert, and not containing any nutrient value. Their sole purpose in life is to hold plants upright and give their roots a way to wander that still exerts needed pressure to the same roots so that they grow root hairs. Quoting the manufacturers, they consider "clay to be an ecologically sustainable and re-usable growing medium because of its ability to be cleaned and sterilized, typically by washing in solutions of white vinegar, chlorine bleach, or hydrogen peroxide, and rinsing completely."

BOTTLE BRUSHES

Bottle brushes are a necessity, as you will appreciate if you've ever tried to clean containers with rolled-up paper towels. If you have none on hand, bottle brushes are available at chemical supply outlets and at most hardware stores.

MIST SPRAYER

Many of the tropical plants enjoy an occasional spray with a mist of warm water. It's an effective way of cleaning a leaf, and red spider mites (which see) have an extreme dislike of water drops.

WATERING CAN

Preferably, your watering can should have a long spout. It will allow you to reach containers in the back row and to pour accurately, thus avoiding spills.

WATER

Your water supply is not overwhelmingly critical. Many indoor water gardeners get good results with tap water (as long as it isn't icy cold). But there are two things to watch out for: well water and chlorinated water, both usually found in most city water systems.

Begin testing for oxygen in your well water by pouring a glass full of liquid from the tap, then set it aside. If bubbles eventually form on the inside of the glass there is oxygen present, but if the water remains bubble-less, you will have to aerate. You can use an aquarium aerator to do the job or pour the water back and forth from one glass to another, not the easy way if you need a lot of water.

For best results, keep an eye on the acidity and chlorine levels of your water. You should have a simple pH measuring tape, which should be available from most aquarium shops. The scale runs from pH 3 (very acid) to pH 7 (neutral) and on up to pH 9 (very alkaline).

Most plants prefer water between pH 6 and pH 7. If your water is too alkaline, collect a gallon in a clean vessel, and add a few drops of vinegar. Test again. When you arrive at the right mixture, make a note for future reference. If the water is too acid (which is unlikely), add a few drops of a solution of bicarbonate of soda. I might add that I found the pH rating to be critical only with the umbrella plants.

The greatest danger in municipal water is chlorine. However, it will work its way out of standing water in a day or two. If your family can do without the bath for a while, run hot water to a depth of about 3 inches (7.6 cm), and let it sit for thirty-six hours. (No other container in the house has so large a surface area.)

Never use water softened by a home appliance. Water softeners work by means of an exchange of chemicals; the result may be pleasant to bathe in, but the plants hate it.

Rain-water and snow are excellent, although if collected in heavily urban areas, they will have absorbed chemicals and particles while flakes fall through the air. I must confess that, when living in the city, I used city rain-water all the time with no adverse effects. Of course, use fresh, clean rain-water and freshly fallen snow. With snow, remember that it takes several shovels full to make an adequate supply of water.

Another method is to keep a large crock of water on hand so that you always have a couple of gallons of chlorine-free water ready to use.

CHARCOAL

Charcoal is an aquarium supply item and is used to absorb gases from decaying vegetation (odors as well). I've never found that it is absolutely necessary to add it to any of my containers, but I always do to be on the safe side.

PLANT FOOD

Most garden books and house-plant manuals give recipes for making one's own plant food. It's not hard to do, but it does require shopping around to find the chemicals needed, and then you must have a place to store them.

Another way is to buy one of the commercially prepared soluble fertilizers now readily available. Most any will do except for one variety that turns the solution blue (unless you like blue water).

Mix a quart or more ahead of time according to the instructions on the powder container so that a mixed supply is always on hand. A good rule: cut the powder instructions by half. It is far better to underfeed than overfeed. Remember that most of the plants that I list don't need food to survive, but with some food they all will grow a bit faster. This becomes the "nutrient solution" that I mention below. Look for a simple 20-20-20, a general purpose fertilizer for maintaining plants in almost any environment. Keep the mix in a cool place in a screw-top bottle so no air gets in to evaporate any of the solution.

Most plants will do very well in water culture without worrying about adding nutrients. But after two or three months, make it a habit that, when topping off evaporated water, add a few tablespoons of your prepared nutrient water to the mix and make a note of the date in your notebook.

LIGHT

Next to water, when growing any houseplants indoors, light is a most important consideration. First, light intensity is measured in foot candles (FC). One FC is the amount of light cast on a white surface by one candle, one foot away, in an otherwise dark room. The size of the candle is relatively unimportant; it's the size of the wick that counts and contributes most to the size of the flame. But for general purposes, consider the candle to be anything between a birthday candle and one generally stuck in a Chianti bottle at an Italian dinner. You can measure FCs with a photo exposure meter or look up an FC conversion table on the web.

Plants like cactuses and most flowering annuals need full sun, which means 6,000 to 8,000 FC. Plants like ferns and begonias, and most of the plants growing in water, prefer partial shade or an average of 2,000 FC. Some plants that grow deep in the jungle need full shade, measuring between 100 and 500 FC.

Windows immediately cut down on light intensity with the loss of light through outside refraction of the glass and the fact that some light is actually absorbed by the glass. Now add architectural details such as eaves and cornices, and more light is lost. A west window in mid-morning may read 400 FC at the inside sill, but only 10 FC six feet into the room, while the outside reading might be over 10,000 FC. If windows are lightly curtained, screened, or dirty (a major problem for the city dweller), more light is lost. Now add a layer of dust to the leaf tops, and the amount of light received by the plant is dim indeed.

I've listed light requirements in terms of sun, partial shade, and shade. Sun needs a window to the south, or truly bright light, for at least four hours a day. Partial shade means an east or west window, while shade is a north window.

PLANTS UNDER LIGHT

With the dawn of the twenty-first century, the entire concept of electric lights has changed; where once there were five types of bulbs at the variety store or box store, today the kinds of bulbs available measure in the hundreds.

But if you find that windows are not enough, you might look into the method of growing plants under artificial light. You could start with a simple hanging fluorescent fixture and, as needs increase, move on up to high-intensity systems or special grow lights that are engineered to help out with seed starting, rooting cuttings, or even providing the additional light needed to keep a special orchid alive through the dark of the winter. One such source is http://www.planetnatural.com/, but there are many more listed in Sources of Supply, page 87.

FIRST STEPS

If your new plant is a cutting, it's ready for the water and can go straight into the dip as is. This is also a very cheap and easy way of getting plants—beg a few six- to eight-inch snips off of a friend, and soon they will show roots and begin to grow.

If your plant comes in a pot with soil, turn the pot over, and, holding the plant stem and dirt with one hand, knock the side of the pot with your other hand. If the dirt sticks in the pot, knock the rim of the pot on the edge of a table. Unless the soil is very wet, a clump of earth surrounding the roots will loosen and fall out. Plastic pots can, if necessary, be cut with a pair of scissors and removed in pieces, the same method being used if the pot is clay.

Now take the ball of earth, place it in a clean pan of tepid water, and let it soak until the earth falls away from the roots. Do this a second time until the roots are quite clean, being very careful to prevent unnecessary damage. Plant roots growing in soil have tiny root hairs extending from the larger roots, and they are easily sheared off if care is not taken removing the soil. Rinse the roots under a gentle flow of tepid water.

Next, take a container and put a few small pieces of charcoal in the bottom, then add the plant and enough plain water to cover the roots and the bottom part of the stem. Never let any leaves remain under water or they will surely rot. Don't forget the charcoal; it is important because it will help to keep the water clear and pure. If you have a wood-burning fireplace, you have ample charcoal on hand. Otherwise find it at pet stores.

The above procedure is fine for Chinese evergreens, ivies, dracaenas, cuttings, and the like. But if the plant is to stand alone in the containers, like a papyrus or umbrella plant, you will want to spread the roots gently in well-rinsed gravel, small stones, or crushed black stone from the hobby shops.

After a few days, if needed, top off the evaporated water. You will soon see new white roots beginning to form, and, as the plant becomes acclimatized, top growth should start.

Sometime if you wish to move rooted plants from a water solution back to dirt in a pot, remember that many plants have two kinds of roots: those that grow in water and those that grow in soil. So remove your plant from the water, and put it in a pot, but add damp sphagnum moss or sand, instead of dirt, keeping the mix damp. After about two weeks, replace the moss or sand with potting soil and resume regular watering. The nature of the roots will change.

CHANGING WATER

If your plants are doing well, don't bother to change the water unless you have an unpleasant accumulation of algae or some dead roots that should be removed. At least once a month, however, change your solutions entirely by pouring off all the water, because the plant roots do need oxygen from the air or fresh water. Although a container with a large surface area will allow a certain amount of oxygen to enter the water by diffusion, and the fresh water you add will contain more oxygen, it's always a good idea to have a complete change. Some water gardeners use bicycle pumps or aquarium aerators to pump oxygen bubbles through the solution every week or so.

NOTEBOOK

It's always a good idea to keep a record of the day the plants are received, where a particular plant came from, when you have decided to increase or decrease the use of the nutrient solution, whether a plant does better in one light source or another, the effects of different temperatures, and so on. You always think you'll remember because it seems so important at the time, but the memory soon fades, and you may have to begin that particular experiment over again.

CLEANING DUST AND PESTS

Even in a well-ordered home, everything gets dusty, and plant leaves are no exception. Dust on leaves does nothing to help the plant, because it cuts down on needed light.

Use a camel's hair brush for occasional brush-offs, and soap and water if the leaves of any plant become layered with grime, which can easily happen even in cities with a good reputation for controlling air pollution. In cleaning your plants, don't be afraid to use a mild solution of soap and tepid water. It won't hurt the plant as long as everything is finally rinsed with clean water. Never use cold water.

GREENFLY OR APHIDS

Aphids can run into the thousands produced by just one aphid birth mother. These are plant sap suckers, and when they are at work, you will notice new growth becoming distorted. They can be removed fairly easily by washing and spraying with water. Most insecticidal soaps will also take their toll.

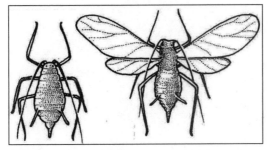

∧ A typical aphid at left and one of the flying variety that enables them to really move.

RED SPIDER MITES

These critters are almost invisible spider-like creatures, reddish or transparent, which spin fine webbing that may entirely coat the underside of affected leaves. If your plant leaves are going yellowish or curiously mottled, suspect there are spider mites at work, and scan the undersides of the leaves with a magnifying glass, where you will readily see the pests if present. Regular washing and mist-spraying deter these insects, but also they will succumb to one of the insecticidal soaps.

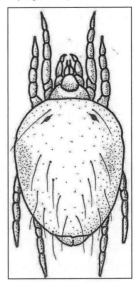

∧ In life a spider mite is about the size of a large period at the end of a sentence. Above it is magnified for detail.

∧ Here are typical spider mites making webs
and destroying leaves and stems.

SCALE INSECTS

Brown scale insects are relatives of greenflies and have the ability to crawl up and down plant stems until they find a place of
comfort. Once stationary, they proceed to create little homes
like domed "scales," usually brownish in color. The domes are
sticky and a result of excretions the insects produce. Another
member of the clan is the dreaded mealy bug, again a small
insect that crawls and is covered with a white, waxy coat. It,
too, leaves behind a sticky residue. Both scales can be rubbed
off the stems using a soft cloth wetted in soapy water or a small
paintbrush or Q-tip dipped in mentholated spirits. For a last
resort, try one of the insecticidal soaps.

WHITE FLIES

White flies are min-
ute white insects that
resemble fluttering
moths and have the
ability to multiply
with a speed that far
exceeds what you
might expect from
their size. As fly
numbers increase,
you will notice they

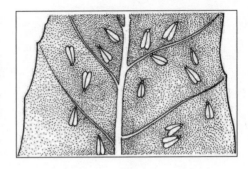

∧ White flies cavort on the undersides of leaves
and suck the life out of plants.

leave behind a sticky residue that coats the leaves of the infected
plant. They are difficult to remove, but the amount of lethal spray
needed makes me a bit nervous. Luckily, you will find on the web a
few manufacturers of nontoxic yellow sticky traps. Small pieces of
yellow cardboard—about the size of a business card—are coated
with glue that doesn't dry out, and the flies stick to the cards and
flutter their last. You hang the cards on the plants.

3

Plants for Your Indoor Water Garden

The following is an informal description of plants that I have tried in my home and found suitable for water gardens and have needed a minimum of fuss. There are, I'm sure, many, many more, and an amazing number of plants will respond to hydroponics when properly potted and tended. Even some cactuses do well in water.

However, for our present purposes, we are concerned with those plants that will do well in plain water or a mild nutrient solution, that require no specialized environments or intricate routines of care, and that will adapt to interesting and decorative containers that can be readily moved around a busy home.

I've listed the plants alphabetically by common name, followed by their scientific name (in Latin), and added brief descriptions. At the top of each entry, you will find temperature and light information, as, for example, "warm/partial shade" or "cool/sun." There is plenty of information on the qualities of light in chapter 2.

TEMPERATURE

Cool ranges from 40°F (Fahrenheit) or 04°C (Celsius) to 50°F or 10°C. These temperatures refer to *night-time* only. Most plants need a drop in temperature at night for healthy growth.

Average indoor *daytime* temperatures can go into 80°F (27°C) up to 90°F (30°C) without adverse effects, but when it comes to winter in parts of the country where winter truly means cold, try to avoid very dry air produced by a high level of heating from radiators or, in England, electric bar fires.

Regarding the lower temperature ranges, if you turn your heat down at night there should be no problems. If you turn the heat down when you go away on a trip, your water plants will do well for a week or two as long as the temperature doesn't go too far below 50°F. If you plan to leave your house on the cool side, move your most sensitive plants away from being close to window glass.

DESCRIPTIONS

An informal description of each genus and each individual species, with the scientific names given in Latin, are listed. When ordering plants, always use the scientific name because common names not only change from the East Coast to the West Coast, they often change from country to country. There is only one scientific name, and generally speaking, most catalogs list plants using the Latin name to avoid confusion.

An asterisk (*) indicates that the plant is illustrated either with a drawing or an image in the color section. I've chosen to illustrate only plants that are or have been in my collection. Each is drawn from life, an experience that has helped me to provide some shadings and textures that are not usually shown. I also drew each plant in a different kind of container as a means of suggesting the virtually infinite variety that you can find at the stores or find in your own home.

The illustrations also show the plant and container in correct proportion and note that the container bottoms are wide enough to prevent an accidental knock-over. Small plants measure between six inches and a foot; medium plants, between one and two feet; and large plants, over two feet tall.

(*) ARROWHEADS, *SYNGONIUM*

Medium/Warm/Partial Shade

Arrowheads are creeping or climbing vines with shiny leaves generally shaped like arrowheads, which seem to thrive even when tossed into an old bottling jar and left for weeks in a dark corner. They're excellent plants for a coffee table or bookshelf, but they like a bright but shaded area in the summertime. When they begin to climb, I generally use nylon fishing line for a support, one end tied to a stone and placed in the container and the other end tacked to the

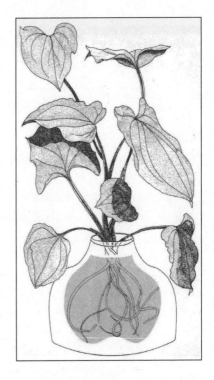

∧ African evergreen

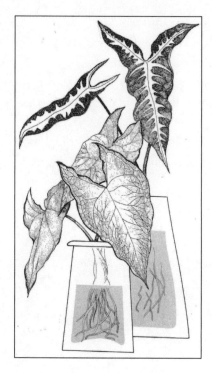

window frame or wall. They are sometimes sold under the name *Nephthytis*. You may not be able to find all the varieties listed, but they give a good idea of the range.

S. auritum: Three-to five-fingered leaves of dark green. A good climber; sometimes called the five-fingered vine.

(*) S. 'Butterfly': has leaves with wavy edges, and the plant truly resembles a host of butterflies.

∧ [Top] Arrowhead plant
[Bottom] Trileaf Wonder

S. macrophyllum: The big-leaf *syngonium* has large, emerald-green, heart-shaped leaves; also a climber.

(*) S. podophyllum: African evergreen is usually found in the juvenile state as a small plant with thin, green, arrow-shaped leaves that become rounded as the plant matures.

S. podophyllum 'Albolineatum': Arrowhead vine. The leaves are divided into five or eight sections of a velvety green, with white edging along the center and side veins.

(*) S. podophyllum 'Atrovirens': Arrowhead plant. The leaves are pale green to a creamy white on a dark-green background.

S. podophyllum 'Emerald Gem': Arrowhead plant that is a shorter and more compact form of the species.

(*) S. 'Pink Allusion': Here is another beautiful plant with the predominant leaf color of pink.

(*) S. podophyllum 'Trileaf Wonder': The center of the leaf is generally a light green deepening toward the edges.

S. wendlandii: Another more compact member of the genus, with deep green leaes and sharply contrasting white veining.

(*) BEEFSTEAK BEGONIA, *BEGONIA*

Large/Warm/Partial Shade

Begonia is both the common name and the generic name for a large collection of mostly tropical plants that have given rise to one of the most popular summer bedding plants, the annual *Begonia semperflorens* hybrids; truly beautiful hanging basket plants, the tuberous begonias; and a number of fanciful cultivars with glorious leaves, including the time-honored rex begonia.

I have one or two plants in my various collections that have been around our house

∧ Beefsteak begonia

for years, and one is the beefsteak or pond-leaf begonia (*Begonia X erythrophylla*), brought to me by my sister-in-law some twenty-five years ago.

I've still got the plant; today it resides in a self-watering pot (it measures a foot across and was called a French Riviera Self-Watering pot, which I bought in Manhattan in 1968), from which it's been repotted thrice, and now the stem—or, more correctly, the rhizome—has again twirled around and around itself in such a complicated configuration that I must surely repot it again. The pot itself has a spigot where water can be poured into the potting mix of sphagnum moss and bird gravel—which has also been changed.

For a houseplant companion to go on year after year with a minimum of care is something of a rarity. In February, the plant flowers freely with lovely pink flowers, and it enjoys a moist planting mix of the aforementioned sphagnum moss and bird gravel. Once a month—except from December to February—it gets a monthly shot of the nutrient solution.

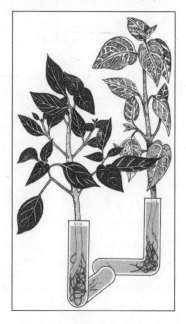

∧ [Top] Yellow bloodleaf
[Bottom] Common red bloodleaf

(*) BLOODLEAF, *IRESINE*

Medium/Cool/Sun

These plants are a decorator's delight; not only are the leaves a vivid shade of magenta that sparkles in the sun, but the veins and stems are also red. The plant develops best in sunlight with the addition of some nutrient to the water, but keep the containers shaded, as the bloodleaf, as do all the other plants, dislike hot water.

(*) *I. herbstii*: Bloodleaf.

(*) *I. lindenii formosa*: The yellow bloodleaf has leaves of yellow, with light-green areas between the veins all on red stems.

(*) BROMELIADS, *TILLANDSIA*

Small/Cool to Warm/Sun or Partial Shade

Bromeliads come in two basic types: epiphytes that live aloft in trees and terrestrial plants with well-developed root systems. All share one characteristic that differentiates them from other plants: the presence of scales on the leaf surface that absorb water and minerals from rain, dew, fog, or mist. This means bromeliads can be houseplants with nothing except something to hold the roots—so they join this book as plants that have, for whatever the reason, forsworn dirt.

Tillandsia are epiphytes and covered with the aforementioned scales, their poorly developed root systems functioning as holdfasts. Because of these scales, most epiphytic bromeliads are extremely adaptable to variations in water, and easily survive in overheated rooms if they are misted every day or two, using a small mister like the type used to dampen clothes for the iron. A monthly shot of nutrient solution to the growing medium is very beneficial.

From time to time, these bromeliads will bloom with small, straight clusters of various colors: pink, red, purple, lilac, or violet.

Probably, the most common member of Tillandsia is the old Southern favorite, Spanish moss (*T. usneoides*). From a distance, it resembles hanging lichens or moss, but if you look closely, you'll see one-inch leaves on threadlike stems and countless silvery scales. Tiny single flowers with chartreuse or blue petals appear on short stalks coming from the leaf axils. It doesn't like cold temperatures and if hung in a window must be misted every day.

The first illustration shows a piece of weathered log, found after a lumbering operation after an independent logger ruined most of the trees growing in a nearby woodland. Rain, wind, and sun had turned the surface to a cracked and pitted silver-gray. By drilling three-quarter- and one-inch-diameter holes about two inches deep, and packing them with sphagnum moss, I have a beautiful and naturalistic setting for seven *Tillandsia*.

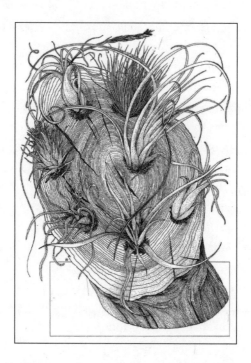

∧ *Tillandsias* mounted in holes drilled in a log.

T. balbisiana: This plant has sixteen-inch twisting leaves arising from a bulbous base. They are a light green with powdery scales.

T. circinnata: Sends up eight-inch, gray-green, twisted leaves from a bulbous base. The scales are a powdery gray.

T. fasciculata: Exhibits the common gray-green, twisted leaves that will grow up to forty inches long.

T. ionantha: Bears dense clusters of three-inch leaves, light green and covered with silvery scales. The origin is Mexico.

T. pruinosa: Is a small plant that looks like a green plush octopus standing on its head. The leaves are three to four inches long, the total plant topping five inches.

T. setacea: Resembles tufts of pine needles up to ten inches in length. The color is dark green in the shade but turning reddish-brown with increased light.

T. valensuelana: Boasts a rosette of light-green leaves with silvery scales growing to twenty inches.

The second illustration shows five bromeliads growing on a piece of forest driftwood, anchored in a six-inch clay pot layered with first sphagnum moss, covered with a layer of bird gravel. This tree goes outside in summer, with from the afternoon sun. The *Dykia* and *Cryptanthus* (see below) are planted at the base because of their terrestrial nature. Others are wrapped in balls of osmunda (dried ferns generally used for housing orchids) and tied to the wood with nylon thread. Bring inside before frost, and handle like the *Tillandsia* log.

Billbergia pyramidalis: Grows as either an epiphyte or a terrestrial. The plant shown is young, and leaves are less than a foot long. As it grows older, leaves will reach two feet with two-and-one-half-inch width. Color is light green with slightly darker stripes running lengthwise. If properly misted, the cup will always be full of water.

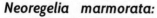
∧ Bromeliads continue to grow after being attached to a log with a dab of super glue.

Neoregelia marmorata: Has pale green leaves up to twelve inches long and two inches wide, marbled with reddish brown. The leaf tips are a brilliant red, hence the common name of the fingernail plant. A flower will occasionally nestle in the vase of the plant.

Orthophytum saxicola: This is a small plant, rarely exceeding five inches in diameter. Leaves are bronze in color, edged with soft spines. Occasional flowers are white.

Dyckia encholirioides: A rosette of bright green leaves edged with spines eventually grows up to eighteen inches long. The leaf undersides are finely traced with silvery gray pencil-like lines. Flowers are orange on a two-foot spike. This is a terrestrial plant, so I planted it on the surface of the gravel, but I'm sure it would do well wrapped in osmunda and tied higher in the tree.

Cryptanthus bivittatus: Is a member of an interesting group of terrestrial bromeliads with the common name of earthstar. My plant has six-inch leaves with piecrust edges. Leaf colors are pink, the edges separated with a band of pale green. The undersides are reddish brown.

After flowering, most bromeliads will die but not before they send up offshoots, which are easily rooted for new plants.

The common pineapple fruit will produce a handsome house plant. Cut off the top growth from a fresh pineapple, taking about an inch of the fruit. Let the cut air-dry for a few days, then root the cutting in moist sand or peat moss. Move the fledgling plant to a five-inch pot of a mix of peat moss and bird gravel, adding water when the mix is dry.

(*) CHINESE EVERGREENS, *AGLAONEMA*

Medium to Large/Warm/Partial Shade

Chinese evergreens are a perennial favorite for water culture. This is another group of plants for poorly lit coffee tables and corners, but they do occasionally require a change to better light. I have a pewter Chinese evergreen that is almost three feet tall and still going strong. Grouped together in a plain battery jar (see page 82), Chinese evergreens are very attractive

∧ Pewter Chinese evergreen

and graceful, and even if named varieties may be difficult to obtain locally, any variety is worth having. Occasionally, obviously prompted by their environment, many will bloom with a strange blossom that immediately points to their relations in the Arum family, in which we find peace lilies and our own Jack-in-the-pulpit (*Arisaema triphyllum*).

A. commutatum elegans: Variegated evergreen. A deep shiny green, spear-shaped leaf with an off-white feathered design.

A. commutatum maculatum: Silver evergreen. Spear-shaped leaves as much as eight inches long with splotches of silvery gray, ash-green to white on a shiny green background.

(*) **A. commutatum 'Pewter':** Pewter evergreen has spear-shaped leaves up to eight inches long, with splotches of silvery gray, ash-geen to white, on a shiny green background.

(*) **A. commutatum 'Red Edge' or 'Syng Pink':** This is a true beauty, and, according to the heritage of the plant you have, the leaves have pink to red blotches and are heavily edged with red.

A. modestum: The familiar Chinese evergreen, with deep green, shiny leaves, found in most plant shops.

(*) COLEUS, *COLEUS*

Medium to Large/Warm/Sun

For generations, *Coleus*, also called painted nettle or flame nettle, has been one of the more important and popular bedding plants for parks, gardens, and home landscapes. It also makes a great houseplant as long as you have good lighting. Every year, the nursery industry offers new coleus cultivars to the market, and there seems to be no end in sight. The leaves are rounded, pointed, ruffled, small or large, and come in every color of the rainbow except blue and the flowers try to make up for this lack by being blue. The stems are square. And because this plant roots with such ease, even from shorter than they should be cuttings, any garden friend will be sure to donate some to your cause. Remember, a grouping of the plants resembles an exotic salad.

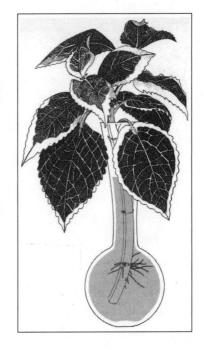

∧ *Coleus* 'Brilliancy'

The leaves need bright light for color intensity, and the addition of some nutrient to your own plants is always beneficial. Pinch off the blooms because they really are of no interest compared to the leaves, and pinch back new growth occasionally to promote new and bushier plants.

Three cultivars called 'Peter's Wonder', 'Hipsters Zooey', and 'Religious Radish' appear in the color images in the insert.

(*) CORN PLANT, *DRACAENA*

Medium to Large/Warm/Sun

Corn plants are so called because the leaves resemble the leaves of corn and have always been popular house plants that seem to grow without constant watching or much in the way of care. With their seemingly endless variety of leaf forms, it's difficult to believe that they all belong to one group of plants. Corn plants are the most popular of the many varieties because of their broad striped rosette of leaves topping a thin trunk.

∧ Striped dracaena, *Deremensis* 'Warneckeii'

(*) ***D. deremensis* 'Warneckeii':** Striped dracaena is my favorite of the group, a handsome plant with long, sword-shaped leaves of bright green, with a light green center stripe, a milky white over-glaze, and pure white edges. It can put up with very poor light for an amazing length of time.

***D. draco*:** Dragon tree. Not at all common, but perhaps you can find one in the home of a friend who has a lot of houseplants. This corn plant has a thick, fleshy rosette of leaves that grow about two feet in length.

***D. fragrans* 'Massangeana':** The original corn plant with yellow and green striped leaves that arch like corn leaves found in a corn field.

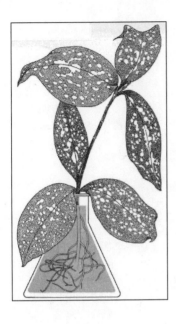

∧ Gold-dust dracaena

(*) *D. godseffiana*: Gold-dust dracaena: A small shrub-like plant with oval leaves that resemble a Jackson Pollack painting with their overall patterns of white spots.

***D. goldieana*:** Queen of Dracaenas: A spectacular plant having broad sword-shaped leaves with horizontal bands of greenish white.

***D. hookeriana*:** Leather dracaena. Dark green rosettes of thick, leathery leaves that are as tough as they look. Not common.

(*) *D. marginata*: Madagascar dragon tree. You will invariably find this plant back-lighted in office buildings and modern theatre lobbies; its rosettes of thin, shiny leaves edged with red ride atop twisted trunks that may grow to ten or fifteen feet under favorable conditions. Very graceful and sculptural; will tolerate poor light.

(*) *D. braunii (D. sanderiana)*: Ribbon plant (page 37) is native to Cameroon in West Africa. The species is a tough and reliable plant for soil or water culture, having leaves that actually resemble shiny ribbons of a deep green with broad to narrow edgings of white or yellowish white.

∧ Madagascar dragon tree

(*) **D. braunii (D. sanderiana)** **'Lucky Bamboo':** For a few years now, a variation on the common species has wended its way throughout the world of box stores, supermarkets, and florists, happily called the lucky bamboo (but bamboo it is not). The labels usually attached to this plant refer to the intertwined stems being topped with leaves as echoing the thoughts usually associated with Eastern mysticism, so often found in New Age culture. Lucky bamboos are popular *Feng Shui* plants. The twisted shapes are produced by rotating

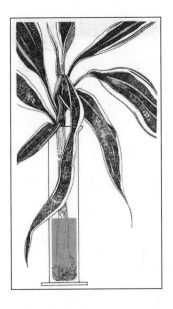

plants with strong light from various angles, a process that is easy for the nurseries that produce these plants but a bit difficult for most home users.

∧ Ribbon plant

(*) CROTON, *CODIAEUM*

Large/Warm/Sun

Commonly known as crotons, most books list the genus as *Codiaeum*, but neither name does any justice to the spectacular foliage of this plant originally from the monsoon areas of the South Pacific. There are many species, but the only one found in cultivation is usually

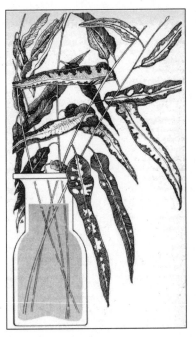

∧ Croton 'Johanna Coppinger'

C. variegatum pictum, and all the croton hybrids have been developed from this parent. In fact there are a couple of hundred cultivars based on the fantastic color variations found in the foliage of these plants. Remember, because they belong to the Euphorbiaceae or spurge family, the milky sap produced by these plants can be considered toxic (although doses must be far more than most would eat) and can cause skin allergies to some people.

Without full sun and temperatures generally above 55°F (15°C), you might have problems with this tropical beauty, but any effort on your part to provide what's needed will be worth it. The branches will last for months in water but will not always root, and when they do, the water temperature must be kept above 68°F (20°C).

There are a great many different forms of croton, varying greatly in leaf shape, patterning, and color. Colors may include red, orange, yellow, and green with some leaves being ribbon-shaped and others, broad and deeply lobed.

The cultivar pictured is *Codiaeum variegatum pictum* 'Johanna Coppinger'.

(*) DUMBCANES, *DIEFFENBACHIA*

Medium to Large/Warm/Partial Shade

Dumbcanes are not only great to look at but have unexpected qualities that most people never know but are hinted at with the common name of dumbcane. Depending on your point of view, dumbcanes have certain characteristics revolving around a chemical contained in the leaves and plant tissues that can cause pain and swelling to human skin, and the leaves, if chewed, render the ingestor speechless. The chemicals are the highly toxic crystals of calcium oxalate, concentrated in the leaves. Calcium oxalate is derived from oxalic acid, and enzymes are released that instigate the release of histamine into the blood. Folklore reports that Indians of the Amazon used the sap on poisoned arrows. So keep this plant out of the reach of children.

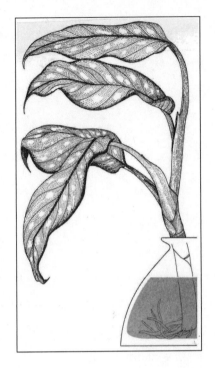

∧ Golden dumbcane

D. amoena: Giant dumbcane. A very large and handsome plant with glossy, oblong, pointed leaves, deep green and covered with yellowish white bands and splotches. A gardener friend had this plant in her living room. When it reached the ceiling, it made a right-angle turn and proceeded to grow horizontally until the weight cracked the cane at about the five-foot level. This is one durable plant!

(*) **D. picta 'Rudolph Roehrs':** Golden dumbcane has leaves of a yellowish-green, with creamy-white splotches.

D. oerstedii: A smaller species with mat green leaves.

D. oerstedii variegata: Leaves of a dark green with a white midrib.

(*) DWARF UMBRELLA-SEDGE, *CYPERUS*

Small to Medium/ Warm/Partial Shade

The dwarf umbrella-sedge is a member of a large family that includes the original papyrus plant that was used for making paper about 3,000 years before the birth of Christ. A grouping of these plants in an old battery jar makes a welcome sight, and some, with proper care, grow quite large and are very imposing. The roots of the plants from the Nile River were used in making *kyphi*, a medical incense of Ancient Egypt.

∧ Umbrella plant

Occasionally, the tips of the leaves turn brown, and I've been told that the pH of the water causes the problem. If too acid, the plant reacts because water for hydroculture should have a neutral pH of 7. Check this with an aquarist's pH tape, or see if somebody at the local high school or technical college can steer you to some litmus paper.

C. albostriatus (formerly called C. diffusus): The dwarf umbrella-sedge has three-sided stems that are triangular if cut in half and bear a rosette of bright-green grass-like leaves on generally foot-high stems. In the spring, brownish-green flowers that resemble small nutlets appear in tufts above the leaves. *'Variegatus'* bears a number of thin white stripes running to the tip of the otherwise green leaves.

(*) FIBER-OPTIC PLANT, SCIRPUS

Small/Cool/Partial Sun

Meet another member the Cyperaceae group (the other being Egyptian papyrus) that has enjoyed great success as a houseplant, especially in Europe, and is known as the fiber-optic plant or *Scirpus cernuus.* The genus is from an old Greek name for a rush first used by Pliny.

The common name of fiber-optic is more apt, and two other common names are fountain bullrush and electric grass. The little white

∧ Fiber-optic plant

primitive flower heads resembling white puffs are found at the tip of each curving stem, while the stems look like ten-inch green threads.

(*) HAWAIIAN TI, *CORDYLINE*

Medium to Large/Warm/Partial Shade to Medium Sun

The Hawaiian Ti plant has a number of common names, including baby doll Ti, Ti-leaf, of just the good luck plant, and is often found in souvenir shops in the Islands or in Florida where it appears as a small three- to four-inch branch in a plastic baggie. The scientific name is now *C. fruticosa* and was once *C. terminalis.*

In the warmer parts of the world, it's a palm-like tropical shrub that can reach a height of about ten feet, but as a houseplant, it grows much smaller. The

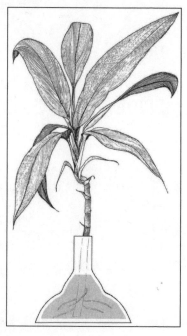

∧ Hawaiian Ti

leaves are about a foot long and exhibit shades of glossy green, reddish purple, or various combinations of white, yellow, red, and purple, appearing in rosettes at the top of the green stems. And there are a host of cultivars, the one in my collection being 'Bicolor'. The Ti came originally from Southeast Asia to Papua New Guinea and was traded throughout the Pacific, where the residents used the starchy rhizomitic roots for food.

Ti plants are easy to propagate from stem cuttings, often called little logs. Cut a mature stem into five-inch sections, remove the leaves, and keep the log on a bed of moist peat moss or sphagnum moss, in a warm place. The green bumps on the stem are called eyes, and each will grow into shoots with leaves. When your cutting produces four to six leaves, you can cut it from the log and root it in water or, again, warm moss.

(*) INCH PLANT, *TRADESCANTIA*

Medium/Warm/Sun

Inch plant, or as it is sometimes called, Wandering Jew, has a long history as an indoor houseplant and an outdoor groundcover, and like biblical folklore, it has a penchant for being an explorer in the garden. Plants bloom with small, three-petalled flowers that last only a day. Some sensitive gardeners find they suffer mild skin irritation from the clear sap in the stems. The scientific name for this plant is presently *Tradescantia* and changed from *Zebrina* some years ago but is still found listed as either in many plant catalogs.

∧ Variegated inch plant

T. pendula: The silvery inch plant is well adapted to hanging containers and has deep green and purple leaves with two silver bands.

T. pendula 'Discolor': This cultivar offers variegated leaves with a reddish-brown background and both purple and silver stripes.

T. pendula 'Quadricolor': The leaf of this cultivar has purple-green leaves banded with white and shaded with pink and red.

(*) IVY, *HEDERA*

Small to Medium/Cool/Sun

Would you believe that there are more than three hundred varieties of ivy available from fanciers and growers? Well, there are, and then some. Many people just collect ivies only, and, when one is aware of the endless leaf varieties and colors, it's not surprising. Mine do quite well in plain water, because I plant them all outside for the summer and then take the best branches for winter cuttings, arranging them in a south window.

There they all look attractive hanging over the edge of various bottles or supported by a simple kind of trellis made from nylon fishing line strung on tacks. An old Chianti bottle hanging on nylon cord in my studio window is filled with Manda's Crested ivy, and on bleak winter days, it's a cheery sight.

Watch out for spider mites, as ivy seems to attract them like dust!

H. canariensis 'Variegata': Canary Islands ivy has a beautiful leaf of slate-green, bluish green, and off-white with a reddish stem. This ivy will adapt to warmer temperatures than the others.

(*) H. helix: English ivy is the best known of the lot and is often used as a groundcover in gardens, where it does have a tendency to spread like wildfire.

(*) **H. helix 'Little Diamond':** A lovely little ivy with inch-long leaves mostly white and spotted with slate and bluish greens.

(*) **H. helix 'Fluffy Ruffles':** This ivy is a baroque delight with its curling ruffled edges, olive-green in color. The young leaves have reddish stems and are edged with a thick mass of short, brownish hairs that become less prominent as the leaf expands.

(*) **H. helix 'Hahn's Self-branching':** A busy little ivy that grows into a compact mass of stems and leaves.

(*) **H. helix 'Manda's Crested':** A star-shaped leaf of jade-green, with rosy edges that busily curl under and grow to about three inches.

(*) **H. helix 'Triton':** A beautiful light green leaf with three to seven long, waving fingers.

∧ Two images of ivy cultivars with close-ups of the leaves on the right. They are, from left to right: 'Manda's Crested', 'Triton', English, 'Little Diamond', 'Fluffy Ruffles', and, on the bottom, 'Hahn's Self-branching'.

(*) IVY TREE, *FATSHEDERA*

Small to Medium/Cool/Partial Shade

This durable and attractive plant, also known as fatheaded Lizzy, is the result of an accidental cross between two plants: the Iris ivy, *Hedera helix hibernica*, and a Japanese Aralia, *Fatsia japonica* 'Moseri', in a French greenhouse before the First World War—a perfect example of the international scope of horticulture. The plant will tolerate very poor light and

∧ Miracle plant

looks fine in a dark hall but needs a summer session outdoors or on a patio to restore its vigor. The leaves can grow quite large (up to eight inches), and it maintains a shrubby growth until it becomes top-heavy. If that happens, tie it up or trim it back.

F. lizei: Ivy tree. This is the original hybrid and has dark green, shiny, five-lobed leaves.

(*) **F. lizei 'Variegata':** Variegated tree ivy has large green leaves mottled with lighter and darker shades of green and edged with white.

(*) JADE PLANT, *CRASSULA*

Small to Medium/Cool/Sun

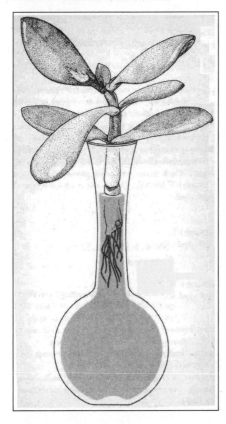

∧ Jade plant

Next to the aspidistra, or the cast iron plant, the jade plant is one of the war-horses of the plant world. Its full scientific name is *Crassula argentea,* and it's one of many kinds of plants that belong to the succulent family. Because this plant is known to survive harsh and dry conditions, it often comes as a surprise to find that the jade will adapt to water culture. I'm still amazed when I see the small roots edge out from the stem-end after a week or two in water.

(*) JAPANESE SPURGE, *PACHYSANDRA*

Medium to Cool/Partial Shade

Everyone who has ever gardened in a city or the suburbs knows about pachysandra because it's used almost throughout America as a ground cover where grass is shunned and maintenance hard to come by. It's an evergreen plant between six and eight inches high, with glossy green leaves and flowering on occasion with small greenish-white blossoms.

Some time ago, I was looking for more plants for the winter, pulled up some pachysandra from the backyard, put it in water, and it has done

∧ Japanese spurge

beautifully. Because this plant is as a groundcover a quick spreader, it's not hard to come by. The full name is *P. terminalis*.

(*) MINIATURE SWEET FLAG, *ACORUS*

Small to Medium/Warm/Partial Shade

As a word, charming is often batted about, but it's a great word to apply to the Japanese sweet flag, and one look will tell

∧ Miniature sweet flag

you why: it looks and it is Japanese. I have grown a cutting in a cordial glass (which in the long run was a mistake because the water evaporated too quickly), but now it's in a larger glass container and easily moved about the house wherever a bit of style is indicated.

A. gramineus pusillus: This is a dwarf form that barely exceeds four inches in height, having swordlike leaves in a fresh green color.

A. gramineus variegatus: Swordlike leaves arranged like a fan with lengthwise stripes of white and green.

***A. gramineus* 'Ogon'**: Has beautiful foliage of light green that is highlighted with bright yellow stripes. Be sure to cut off the old foliage when new leaves arise.

(*) MOSES-IN-THE-CRADLE, *RHOEO*

Small/Cool/Sun

Occasionally known as *Rhoeo discolor* in the florist's trade, this attractive plant is also called the boat lily. The foliage is stiff and waxy with leaves up to a foot long that form a tight rosette about the stem. These leaves are a metallic green above with a deep purple on the undersides. Little white flowers peek from boat-shaped bracts that form at the base of the leaves at unpredictable times of the year, hence the popular names. There is only one species in the genus.

∧ Moses-in-the-cradle

(*) PEACE LILY, *SPATHIPHYLLUM*

Medium/Warm/Partial Shade

For three reasons, the peace lily has maintained its status as a decorator's favorite, not to mention one of the most popular plants grown in the various malls around the country. First, it

∧ A peace lily plant in bloom

blooms almost continually; second, it survives in poor light; and third, aside from being picked and pinched at by mall-walkers, the only other enemy is the mealy bug, and that is easily dispatched. The shiny arrow-shaped leaves on their long and sturdy stalks make an elegant showing, but when you add the white flowers, everyone is impressed.

These plants prefer a winter temperature of not much below 65°F, so a dependable warm spot is needed. They appreciate a daily misting of the leaves, and when potted up, here's another plant that needs its roots surrounded by bird gravel, tiny pebbles, or even—if you can find them—clay pellets.

The cultivar 'Mauna Loa' has the largest flowers.

(*) PHILODENDRONS, *PHILODENDRON*

Small to Medium to Large/Warm/Partial Shade

Meet the stalwart family in houseplant love and lore—an amazing group of plants that can transform a drab bookcase, a dull bedroom, a boring wall, or a trapped-in-time coffee table.

These are basically jungle plants that begin life on dark, moist, spongy ground formed of layers and layers of vegetable debris. As they grow, they climb up the nearest supports—usually tightly-packed tropical tree trunks—striving to reach light that continually filters through the branches above. The ground serves only as a holdfast and short-term feeding post, until the plants have sufficient anchorage to begin their climb. When allowed to trail from the edges of pots, the leaves remain rather small and sparse in growth, but let them proceed up the metaphorical ladder, and you will be amazed at the change.

In an east window of my studio, three philodendrons (burgundy, fiddle-leaf, and cut-leaved) sit in glass jars made from quart beer bottles, suspended by nylon fishing line (see page 84), their stems supported by clear plastic rods. The aerial roots branch out in all directions, and the plants sway whenever someone walks by. The temperature is warm, but by 11:00 AM, the light is dimmed by outside trees, so the plants are as close to their natural habitat as they will ever find. Because in the wild most of the fertilizer these plants receive comes from rainwater trickling down tree trunks, absorbing insect and animal wastes on the way, and in turn being absorbed by the aerial roots of the philodendrons, I fertilize them in much the same way by spraying the leaves and stems about once every three or four weeks with a solution of weak plant food, using a hand mister. I use warm water to simulate jungle humidity, and the leaves are cleansed of their dust accumulations about once a month, usually on a weekend afternoon, while the BBC plays on the radio. These plants sit in plain water, and the plants thrive.

Philodendrons are divided into two groups: the *climbers*, which eventually need some type of support to grow upon, and the *self-headers*, which send out their leaves from a common point so that the stem eventually becomes a trunk.

(*) *P.* 'Burgundy': The burgundy philodendron (page 53) is a compact climber with leathery leaves up to a foot long, shaped like an arrow as they mature; color is deep green, with a red-wine cast and red stems.

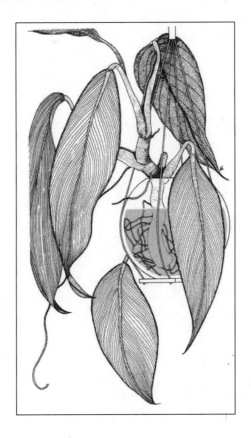

∧ Burgundy philodendron

P. cannifolium: Flask philodendron. A self-header growing with spear-shaped leaves and continually swollen stems.

P. domesticum: Elephant's ear. Good climber and very tropical looking. Green, arrow-shaped leaves that resemble elongated hearts.

(*) *P. scandens*: Heartleaf philodendron. If nothing else ever succeeded in a home, the heartleaf can be trusted. Put it on a bare shelf in the worst light in the room, and this plant will exist, although the leaves will become very small; just give it some support and some light, and you'll be surprised by the change.

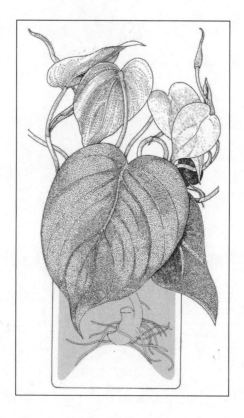

∧ Heartleaf philodendron

(*) _P. panduriforme_: Fiddle-leaved philodendron. This particular species is a very good climber and has leaves that resemble the head of a fiddle.

(*) _P. radiatum_: Cut-leaved philodendron. Also called _P. dubium_ because originally plant collectors were not sure about the correct identification.

∧ Fiddle-leaved philodendron

(*) _P. sodiroi_: Silver-leafed philodendron (page 56). The leaves are a bluish green, with an overall cast of silver. The plant is a climber, and the leaves change shape as the plant matures, becoming larger and prominently veined, but some of the silver tones decrease.

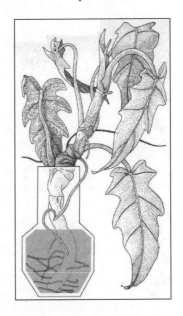

∧ Cut-leaved philodendron

∧ Silver-leaf philodendron

P. wendlandii: Bird's-nest philodendron. A self-header with waxy green leaves sporting a pronounced midrib. The membrane covering the developing leaves is white.

(*) PIGGYBACK PLANT, _TOLMIEA_

Small to Medium/Cool/Partial Shade

    A charming little plant with light, fresh green leaves, somewhat heart-shaped, with cut edges and covered with silky-smooth, small hairs. New plants arise at the base of the leaf, perfect but miniature imitations of the parent. In poor light, the stems become rather long and arching, whereas in good light, the plant becomes bushier and compact; every one of these little plantlets will root, and, I imagine, if one keeps it up, the country might be overrun! Use a nutrient solution. The full name is *Tolmiea menziesii*.

∧ Piggyback plant

(*) PITCHER PLANTS, *SARRACENIA*

Small to Medium Large/Warm/Sun

The first insectivore plant to be carefully examined was the *Sarracenia purpurea*, found and described in North America by an unknown artist around 1550. The botanists and the public of the day were amazed by these plants, and even in the present century, fly-eating plants garner interest in both the scientific press and the supermarket tabloids. Because these plants have poorly developed root systems and are generally found in wet and boggy conditions, high in acidity but deficient in nitrogen, they have developed the ability to self-manufacture food supplies with an occasional treat of live meat. Do not feed them, because they can survive without living food.

When it comes to a container, start with at least an inch of coarse gravel mixed with bits of charcoal. Then add an inch layer of sphagnum moss or peat moss, topped with an inch of sand or, from the craft store, crushed black stone.

I chose the following two plants for the beginning grower, but those of an adventurous mind will probably want to try the original pitcher plant from the past, *S. purpurea*. But if you do, I suggest using an old-fashioned two-gallon glass fishbowl from the variety store.

(*) **S. flava**: This pitcher plant has trumpets that vary from light green to yellow and is found naturally in swamps

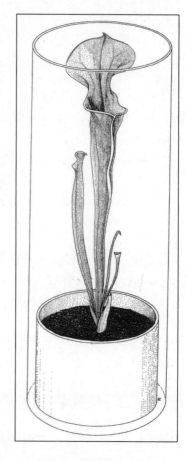

∧ Yellow pitcher plant

from northern Florida to Alabama and southern Virginia. In the accompanying drawing, the plant is growing in a small white ceramic pot, enclosed in an acrylic tube that is four-and-one-half inches in diameter and about a foot high. This is to keep up the humidity level that nature usually provides for these plants.

(*) **S. psittacina**: In nature, the parrot pitcher plant is found in Florida, Louisiana, and Georgia, along the coast. The pitchers begin growth being small and with age reach a length of three to

Fatshedera lizei variegata.

Aglaonema 'Red Edge' or
sometimes 'Thai Christmas'.

Aglaonema 'Red', showing the tangled mass of roots.

Aglaonema 'Red' with a white blossom emerging
through the leaves.

Amazon sword plant and eel grass.

Chlorophytum comosum 'Vittatum'.

Coleus 'Hipsters Zooey'.

Dracaena 'Warneckii'.

Egyptian papyrus: *Cyperus papyrus.*

An ivy cultivar: *Hedera helix* 'Glacier'.

Horsetails: *Equisetum hyemale.*

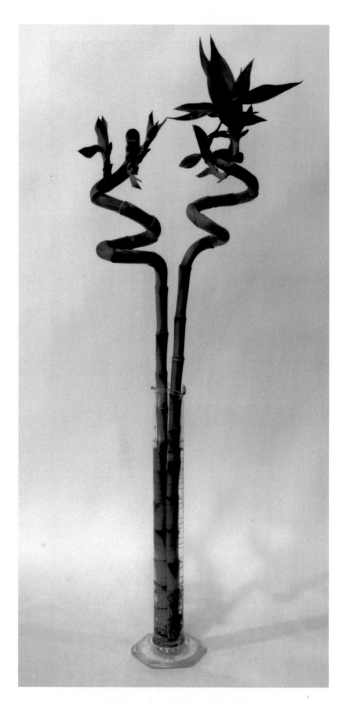

Lucky bamboo: *Dracaena sanderiana*.

Syngonium 'Butterfly'.

Syngonium 'Pink Allusion'.

Philodendron 'Moonlight'.

Parrot pitcher plants with small brass
scorpion: *Sarracenia psittacina*.

Pothos 'Neon'.

From left to right, daffodil bulbs in water showing plenty of roots, Japanese pacysandra, and a small umbrella plant.

Three coleus cultivars, clockwise from top: 'Peter's Wonder', 'Hipsters Zooey', and 'Religious Radish'.

four inches, often tending to lie on the medium provided. Mine are housed in a glass container (see photo page TK) with a layer of sphagnum moss topped by a layer of crushed black stone.

(*) POTHOS, *SCINDAPSUS*

Small to Medium/Warm/Partial Shade

Usually, as plants go, pothos is a seemingly happy vine with one fault: it needs warmth, and, unless it gets at least 60°F, the plant becomes inactive and just sits there. Pothos is fine for table edges or bookshelves, or hanging against walls.

Reasonably good light is required to keep the color of the leaves in good tone, but it's worth the extra effort to find a preferred location.

In tropical locations, the leaves can grow quite large, but in the home, they seem to be contented if they reach a five-inch length. Without support, this vine creeps and trails.

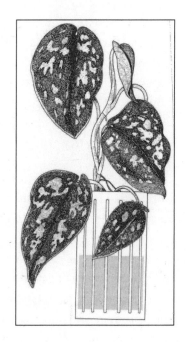

S. *aureus*: Known as devil's ivy and often called golden pothos. Broad, dark green leaves blotched with yellow and having a very waxy look. Pinch stems back if your get tired of the length.

S. *aureus* 'Marble Queen': A variety with many streaks of pure white running through the leaves.

∧ Satin pothos

S. aureus 'Tricolor': The same basic leaf of the other varieties, but the basic green is dappled with yellow, yellowish green, and creamy white.

(*) S. pictus 'Argyraeus': The satin pothos (page 59) boasts a beautiful leaf with a satin-like finish over a bluish-green background completely edged with silver and with random silver markings on the leaf surface.

(*) RUSHES, *JUNCUS*

Large/Cool/Sun

Rushes belong to a rather small family of plants, and their generic name of *Juncus* comes from the Latin word, *juncere*, which also means rush, most likely referring to employing rushes in making furniture seats. Most plants come from cold and barren lands, and in addition to chair seats, they were also used when they were mixed with herbs and flowers then strewn upon floors that rarely benefited from visits with a broom. One of the charges of extravagance leveled against Cardinal Wolsey was "that he caused his floors to be strewn with rushes too frequently."

(*) J. effusus: The primal rush that is found growing across the world, often in cow pastures and marginal swamps. They survive in very poor soil and have pale-green stems that are very pliant and end in a point. They have no leaves except for a few brown wrappings at the base of the plants. Flowers sometimes occur halfway up the stems, forming side-panicles of greenish-brown spikelets. This is obviously one primitive plant. If you peel the green outer layer of the stem, just as you'd pull a zipper, you will find a center core of white pith. Years ago, this was dried, tied with others, then soaked in kitchen grease and lit for rush candles.

(*) *J. effusus* 'Spirilis': This is an unusual cultivar that is just what its namesake describes. The stems become living and green corkscrews that fall gently to the growing medium and twist about in all directions. This is another plant that prefers to have its roots pressing up against something, so my plants are grown in a layer of sphagnum moss topped with black crushed stone—but small pebbles or bird gravel would do handsomely.

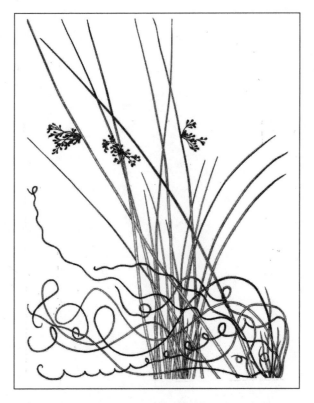

∧ The common field rush is shown with primitive flowers blooming towards the stem tops. The plant at the bottom is called the corkscrew rush.

(*) SCREW PINE, *PANDANUS*

Medium to Large/Warm/Sun

Screw pines resemble palms without trunks. The leathery, sword-shaped leaves grow up the woody trunk in a spiral (hence the common name), and the leaf tip usually ends in a pointed thorn. Keep winter temperatures above 55°F because growth slows down below this minimum.

New plants appear as suckers about the base of the parent plant. When they get to an advanced age, they may produce prop roots, or stilts, from various spots along the stem. In nature, these help to hold the plants erect.

The species usually found in cultivation is *Pandanus veitchii*, which is usually sold in an attractive variegated form.

∧ Screw pine

(*) SONG OF INDIA, *DRACAENA*

Small/Medium to Large/Warm/Partial Shade

Dracaena reflexa (D. pleomeleis) is a most attractive ornamental consisting of a tightly-packed ascending rosette,

tightly wrapping a branching stem that can grow quite tall. The normal form found with some dealers is a variegated variety with the leaves margined with off-white bands, although you can still find the old-fashioned plain green species. This plant is another member of the Dracaena clan, and like most members of the clan, the bottom leaves sometimes turn yellow and fall. This turns out to be the plant's habit of shedding leaves as new leaves appear.

∧ Song of India

(*) SPIDER PLANT, *CHLOROPHYTUM*

Small to Medium/Cool/Partial Shade

Spider plants are time-honored houseplants that have been popular for basket-growing over many years. New plantlets develop on the ends of long, arching, wiry stalks that become pendant as they gain in weight from their developing cargo. The leaves grow between four and eight inches in length and are about half an inch wide and occasionally flower with small, white, and not very distinguished, blossoms—it's the habit of growth that makes this plant so well-liked. Amazingly, over the past few years, gardeners discovered that when offered a spot in well-drained soil and partial shade, the spider plant adapts to outdoor garden culture, especially in the warmer parts of the Southeast.

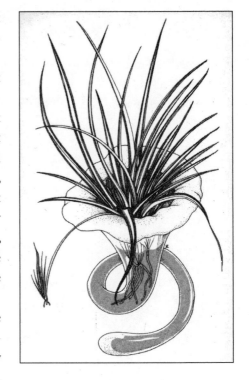

∧ Spider plant

When plants are suited to their environment, many new stalks will appear, all forming small plantlets at the tip, hence the common name. The original plant grew with all green leaves that had a slightly lighter green shade running down the center of the leaf. Its only claim to fame rested with the knowledge that it adapted to darker spots than the three newer cultivars. I think a search would be in the cards if you wanted to find specimens today. Three newer varieties are usually offered for sale.

(*) **C. comosum** 'Vittatum': For decades, this was the most popular variety of spider plants and held its position until the late 1990s. Leaves were mid-green in color with a broad white stripe running down the midrib.

***C. comosum* 'Variegatum':** This cultivar is newer to the market than 'Vittatum', and has dark green leaves with white margins and is generally more compact than the previous plant. The long stems that support the offsets are green. It's a striking plant and has generally replaced the popularity of the 'Vittatum' at nurseries and garden centers.

***C. comosum* 'Bonnie':** This variety has the traditional green with white stripe variegation of 'Vittatum', but its leaves curl and bend. Flowering stems are yellow, and plantlets have curly leaves like the parent. Its best quality concerns the compact size, which is ideal if your home collection is limited in space.

(*) SWEET POTATO, *IPOMOEA*

Small to Medium/Moderately Warm/Sun

This plant is an especial favorite of mine because it wings the mind's eye back to grade school and really basic botany, those days when every family in my ken grew sweet-potato vines in the kitchen window. There was always great excitement when the first roots crept out, and by the time five or six shoots had appeared at the top, it was difficult to return to your Cream of Wheat®.

Well, it's still an exciting plant to grow, and one can become quite inventive when trying to outdo the old toothpick approach. Remember the old instructions? Take an old canning jar half full of water and suspend a sweet potato on four or five toothpicks thrust into the sides so that the bottom of the potato just touches the water. Replace the water as it evaporates. The old way still works, but with all the attractive plastics and new containers available today, why not try to improvise a bit?

When buying a sweet potato, check the tuber for signs of life, because today many of these vegetables are dried for supermarkets, and some tubers will not sprout. Sometimes the local co-op is the best place for good, organically grown vegetables.

While on the subject of vegetables, don't forget that for a short-term plant, look to carrot tops. Cut off the top two inches of a fairly fresh

∧ Sweet potato

carrot, and place it in a dish on wet bird gravels or pebbles so the cut carrot just touches the water. Don't submerge the carrot. Soon the carrot will put forth new growth like it once did in the garden because it's really a root itself.

(*) UMBRELLA TREE, *BRASSAIA*

Medium to Warm/Partial Shade

Large umbrella trees are often seen in the lobbies of some banks, insurance offices, and corporate headquarters; they can grow quite large with a minimum of care. Umbrella trees are among the plants that, if given an open surrounding and air that stays warm in the winter, have the ability to adapt to reduced light. They are originally from the forests of Australia, particularly Eastern Queensland, plus New Guinea and Java.

My present plant was given to me as a seedling and has been in a large glass container. Although not growing terribly fast, it continues to grow slowly and is quite healthy.

The full name is *Brassaia actinophylla*, sometimes listed with the genus *Schefflera*, bearing shiny, palmate (like the fingers of the hand) leaves that are deep green and up to ten inches wide. In jungles, this plant is often found growing as an epiphyte or in various tree crotches of other forest trees. Prune it to control height.

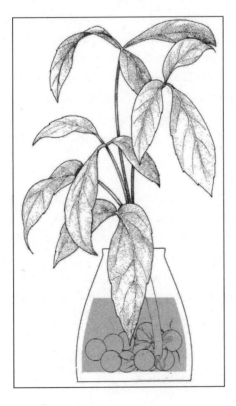

∧ Umbrella tree

(*) VELVET PLANT, *GYNURA*

Medium to Large/Cool/Partial Sun

The look of a velvet plant presages something out of the ordinary, for it could easily be the favorite houseplant of the Wicked Queen in Snow White or perhaps be found growing in the musty basement where the Spider Woman outwitted Sherlock Holmes. The genus is *Gynura* and come from the Greek *gyne*, for female, and *oura*, tail, and refers to the long and rough stigma in the flower, not a very romantic name for a plant with the look of this one. The species name of *aurantiaca* mean yellow-orange and refers to the flower color.

The green leaves and stems are soft to the touch, because they are completely covered with a purple plush, much like the velour that was once used to cover seats in railway passenger cars. And the plants are actually vines and can grow up to eight feet in a good season, but to retain the rich purple coloring, remember to trim back the stems to three feet or less. The cut-off stems can be easily given to friends who can root them in a glass of water.

There is a flower of bright orange, but it has an odor a bit like the contents of a dust bag in your vacuum cleaner, so if you are fastidious, clip it off upon opening.

Like a few plants in my water garden, this one is at home in another old French Riviera Pot, where the soil mix is shredded sphagnum moss mixed with bird gravel and is kept evenly moist from spring to fall, then cut back to drying out between watering until spring arrives.

I have heard stories of this plant wandering a ceiling where support cords have been provided, but I will continue to cut back when necessary.

∧ Velvet plant

OTHER PLANTS TO TRY

Many more plants than those covered in the previous pages will remain fresh in water and often take root. Pussy willows (*Salix* spp.) will leaf out after the catkins, or flowers, have bloomed. Weeping-willow stems will do the same and put out buds and shoots. Periwinkle (*Vinca minor*), makes a most attractive arching fountain of leaves and roots that will often form on many of the stems; start these in spring. Another springtime favorite is the forsythia bush. Before spring flowering, most tree branches will leaf out and blossom in a vase of water when introduced to the warmth of the house. Arborvitae (*Thuja* sp.) branches, rhododendrons, and blueberries (*Vaccinium* sp.) all do well in water-filled containers.

A host of grasses and sedges from marshy and swampy areas will last a season in the house. Water chestnuts (*Trapa natans*), water-fern (*Ceratopteris thalictroides*), and parrot's feather (*Myriophyllum aquaticum)* are all fresh and exciting when displayed in open bowls of water.

(*) UNDERWATER GARDENS

The Amazon sword plant (*Echinodorus brevipedicellatus*), Cape Fear spatterdock (*Nuphar sagittifolium*), or common eel grass (*Vallisneria torta*) are all common underwater plants that can be found at aquarium suppliers and pet stores. They require very little care except for the removal of leaves that have turned brown and an adjustment of light conditions (no direct sunlight). Look for the beautiful (*) Madagascar lace plant (*Aponogeton fenestralis*), a large and very beautiful submerged plant with leaves resembling crochet or macramé embroidery. This plant does not like calcium salts, so provide soft water, only slightly on the acidic side, and try to keep temperatures above 60°F, or it may go into a dormant period.

∧ Madagascar lace plant

When planting a water garden in an aquarium or battery jar, some nutrients must be added to the bottom of the container. First put a thin layer of sand (not beach sand because of the salt), then cover this with an inch-thick layer of bird gravel. Now top it with another thin layer of sand. The three layers should be about three inches deep, sloping up to the rear of your container. Be careful to spread the plant's roots about in the medium.

Other plants to try in an underwater garden are tape grass (*Cryptocoryne ciliata*), water sprite (*Ceratopteris thalictroides*), and water poppy (*Hydrocleys commersonii*), with water lettuce (*Pistia stratiotes*) and azolla (*Azolla caroliniana*) to float on the top.

It's a world of experimentation because many plants that web authorities claim will rot in water do not and, of course, visa versa. Some others only live for a year or so, but the vast majority of plants take to water like ducks, and much of the fun involved in this kind of gardening is the enjoyment in finding and experimenting with new varieties.

4

Bulbs in Water—and One Pit

When the cold winds of winter sweep through the streets of northern cities and snow piles up to the ledges of kitchen windows out in the country, when you're drenched with sleet and icy rains while trudging to the mailbox or general store or corner delicatessen and returning home with a burning hate for nature, nothing is quite so warming and encouraging to the spirit as the sight of spring flowers glowing on a water-filled container on a windowsill or coffee table.

In a process known as *forcing*, you can push bulbs into earlier blooming, and providing spring bulbs that bloom for Christmas is much easier than many people think. While a rich soil may produce a showier flower, it's not necessary; the flower is already formed, small and perfect, covered by the leaf layers of the bulb. *Forcing* is a rather unpleasant name for the process. All you are doing is forcing the bulb to speed up the timetable of the seasons, making the bulb think that December or January is already March or April when it is returned to the warmth of a room.

Two types of bulbs are available: the hardy, outdoor types such as hyacinths, crocuses, and lily-of-the-valley (technically not a bulb but a rootstock called a pip) and the tender bulbs that will not survive a northern winter. The latter are the paper-whites, those known as 'Soleil d'Or' or *Narcissi tazetta*, and two tropical additions, the bulb of the devil's tongue or the so-called Voodoo lily (*Sauromatum guttatum*) and the pit of that common salad treat, the avocado (*Persea americana*).

These bulbs, and that one pit, can all be found in autumn garden catalogs or in garden supply stores, where part of the preparation for winter blooming has already been done for you by the nurseries involved; the bulbs have been preconditioned to bloom early by controlled fluctuations in temperatures. A word of caution: never let any of these bulbs dry out once you've started their growth, for they will not survive such treatment.

(*) HYACINTHS, *HYACINTHUS*

Roman hyacinths bloom a bit earlier than the common hyacinth and have fewer flowers but make up for it with their intense fragrance. Any glass container with sufficient area for root development and a neck that is slightly narrower than the width of the bulb will do. I grow my bulbs in small, graduated cylinders (see page 82) so that the pattern of the roots becomes almost as interesting as the plants.

In forcing, the bulbs must be made to believe that a period of winter has already passed. I use the refrigerator for this deception. Fill the container with water so that it just touches the bottom of the bulb (no higher or the bulb may begin to rot) and set it on the rear shelf of the fridge, perhaps on a piece of cardboard or the like to prevent accidental tipping when the door is slammed. Leave the bulbs for about a month, checking to see that the water level is kept up, and watch for the roots to develop. The bulb must never be allowed to send up leaves or buds without sufficient roots or they will not bloom.

When the white, twining roots have filled the glass container, remove it and place it in a cool, sunny window, rotating the container daily so the flower stalks remain straight as they grow.

I start mine about the first of November and have booms for Christmas and New Year's. By staggering your schedule, you can have flowers for most of the winter. When storing these bulbs for later use, keep them in paper or plastic bags, with holes punched to allow air circulation, in the bottom of the fridge, and make sure they do not become damp or wet during this dormancy or they may spoil.

OTHER VARIETIES OF HYACINTH

Standard large hyacinths come in many beautiful colors: 'L'Innocence': pure white; 'City of Haarlem': yellow; 'Jan Bos': bright red; 'Perle Brilliant': light blue; and 'Pink Pearl': delft blue.

Special hyacinth glasses are often found in antique shops, but today new glasses are offered in many garden catalogs, and recently, plastic containers have appeared on the market. They are shaped much like an hourglass, the upper segment holding the bulb just above the water level, or have a plastic frame with projections to hold the bulb. The procedure is the

∧ Hyacinth in glass.

same for the Roman hyacinth, but these varieties take longer to mature, usually three months from start to bloom.

Remove the glass from the fridge when the jar is filled with roots and the top shoot is about two inches high. Put the jar and bulb in a cool area with an inverted paper cone over the top for about two weeks to prevent the buds from blooming before the stem is long enough. After flowering has commenced, try to keep the plants in a cool spot so the flowers will last longer.

Unfortunately, these bulbs are completely depleted by forcing, and must be discarded after they have bloomed.

(*) LILY-OF-THE-VALLEY, *CONVALLARIA*

That wonderful flower of fragrance and style known as the lily-of-the-valley is often available at the same time as the other bulbs you might force for bloom and usually come preplanted in a special mix to which you just add water. You can, however, save a bit of money by buying the pips and planting them yourself. They can be potted in almost any material that will hold moisture, even sand, but I use aquarium gravel in bowls or dishes at least three inches high.

∧ Lily-of-the-valley

The pips are placed in the gravel or sand with the buds just above the surface, watered thoroughly, and placed in a cardboard box (with holes punched in the sides for ventilation) for about two weeks at room temperature. Then place them in a darkened area of the room for a few days before exposing the plants to bright light.

(*) CROCUS, *CROCUS*

The familiar blues and yellows of crocuses found in early spring are easily grown for indoor bloom. Use a container that is deep enough to allow the roots to develop without pushing the corms out of the gravel. For a showy display, fill with gravel or sand, and set at least six bulbs (corms) on the surface so that the corms will always be out of the water. Add water to just below the top of the medium, and follow the fridge routine. If you use a glass

∧ Crocuses

container, the development of the roots is quite fascinating. Always remember to keep the bulbs in darkness until active root growth is evident, or they will not flower. Crocuses can also be grown in a small glass, like hyacinths, but are not really showy enough to warrant it.

(*) NARCISSUS, *NARCISSUS*

For paper-white narcissus, 'Soleil d'Or', and Chinese sacred lilies, choose containers that are deep enough for root development. Fill two-thirds full with gravel, and add water to the top of the gravel. Then place the bulbs on top of the gravel gently so as not to disturb the bottom of the bulb where the roots will arise, and surround the bulbs with more gravel to keep them upright, leaving the top half clear. Because these bulbs come from gentler climates and are once again specially preconditioned by the growers, they do not require intense cold to start them off.

∧ Soleil d'Or Narcissus

Place them in a cool (50° to 60°F), dark, well-ventilated spot until the shoots are about three inches tall. Move the pot to a lighted area (a north window is perfect) for three or four days, then set the pot in the sunlight. Occasionally, rotate the container so the developing leaves do not aim for the sun. Always keep the gravel moist, but never let the bulbs themselves get wet, only their roots. When my bulbs were planted during the first days of the first of November, the 'Soleil d'Or' bloomed the week before Christmas and New Year's, and the Chinese sacred lilies bloomed the third week of January.

(*) AMARYLLIS, *HIPPEASTRUM*

Surely the queen of the winter window is the amaryllis, one of a number of tropical bulbs that mostly hail from tropical America—and the everybody's instructions always tell you the kind of soil and pot to provide.

But last year I had an extra amaryllis bulb and instead of potting it in soil, I placed the bulb over water, using a thick glass jam gar and a circular support cut from a piece of heavy acetate. Soon the leaves began to grow and the bulb produced long white roots, the tips covered with tiny hairs. In six weeks the bulb produced a stalk and bloomed with three magnificent flowers. Once they had bloomed I cut the stem that held the floral display and moved the jar and plant into a cooler greenhouse where the temperature stayed around 55°F.

I kept it in water, changing the liquid every three weeks and adding a weak solution of liquid plant food once every month. By April the bulb had grown in water for about six months so I removed the bulb from the water and planted it in moist sphagnum moss, them in another month moved it to soil.

∧ These drawings show the following plants growing in water (from left): a Roman hyacinth, crocus, and avocado pit, devil's tongue, Soleil d'Or narcissus, the yet-to-bloom flower of an amaryllis, and another small crocus.

(*) AVOCADO, *PERSEA*

Decide on having an avocado salad for lunch.

Remove the large pit, which is really a seed, from the avocado center then rinse it well with water, using a paper towel to dry it off. Take care that it doesn't slip from your grasp because a wet seed is often very slippery.

Next at the pit's widest part, push three toothpicks into the seed thus enabling you to suspend the pit over a glass (or other container) of water keeping the pointed end straight up and the bottom of the pit just touching the water's surface. Keep the glass and its pit in a warm place, making sure that you maintain the water level where you began. Change the water every week to ten days, especially if you see any algae developing.

In two to six weeks, roots will appear growing into the water and a stem will sprout from the seed with leaves appearing at the tip. When the stem is about six inches long, trim it in half in order to force the fledgling plant into producing more leaves. At his point you can move the pit to a small pot using clean houseplant soil for a medium.

Or you can leave the plant growing in water, and as it gets larger, carefully move it to a larger glass but eventually the pit will give up the ghost and the plant will do better in soil, unless you wish to begin a great experiment and move the plant to a pot filled with clay pellets, as described on page 00, and continue on with hydro-culture.

Remember, if growing an avocado from seed it can take from five to twelve—or more—years to set fruit, and then only if the tree decides to flower.

(*) DEVIL'S-TONGUE, *SAUROMATUM*

Here's one bulb that will bring a great deal of comment—often guarded—to you plant collection. When plants represent the kind of exotic behavior usually assigned with being somewhat odd and strange in their behavior, they reflect that oddness in their discoverer's selection of common names and also have a tendency to hop around when it comes to scientific nomenclature, too. *Sauromatum venosum* is also known as *S.guttatum, Arum cornutum,* and *Typhonium venosum,* with the second most notable part of the plant being the flower. This blossom tops a short stalk and can often reach—when the petal is unfurled—a length of two or more feet, with that single petal about an inch wide. But when grown in water, they stay a bit smaller than found in an outside garden setting.

As it the flower unfurls, the inside of that single petal (technically called a spathe) is blotched with various shades of a heavy violet then streaked with irregular patches of tints featuring a fairly bright yellow-ocher pattern—but the ultimate feature of the flower is its smell.

That scent has been described as being close to the smell of rotting meat or as one hobbyist of the bizarre once told me, resembling the smell of sneakers, unwashed for two or more years, fried in rancid butter, so when it bloom, good taste demands that it goes outdoors. And the smell reflects nature's choice of pollinators for this plant; because there are no honey bees in the various deserts or jungles where it naturally grows, in order to produce fertilized seed, this beauty mist attract only flies.

Once the bloom is finished, allow the bulb to dry out and assuming that you brought it into flower during the summer, and then store for the winter months in a cool and dry place—perhaps in a small box or bag surrounded with dry sphagnum moss and a temperature of about 50 degrees F.

5

All About Containers

Thousands of commonplace and not-so-commonplace objects can make interesting and exciting containers for your plants: old medicine bottles, green wine bottles, and antique milk bottles—to name but a few. In the previous chapters, I have tried to indicate some of the possibilities by drawing each plant in a different shape of container.

You will soon go way beyond these suggestions. An amazing amount of the accumulation of years (upper shelves of a kitchen cabinet, dusty corner of an old attic) can be dragged out and rethought with an idea toward water-plant display. Every time I sit down to think of possible containers, I come up with at least one or two fresh ideas.

CHEMICAL GLASSWARE

Glass containers developed for use in laboratories are often very pleasing. Since the chemist has no time to be bothered with superfluous appendages, appliqué, and gee-gaws (can you imagine what a Victorian test tube might be?), much of it is available at chemical supply houses and can easily be purchased by ordinary buyers. Here are the basic shapes with some guidance for size and capacity (most of this glassware is measured in milliliters).

Battery Jars: Straight-sided cylinders of clear glass available in pints, quarts, and gallons—once used for batteries. A one-gallon jar is about eight inches high and six inches in diameter.

Beakers: Clear glass jars with a lip for pouring. They come in various capacities measured in milliliters. Thirty milliliters equal approximately one ounce. One liter is approximately one quart.

Bottles: Straight-sided with narrow mouth, wide mouth, or extra-wide mouth; usually measured in ounces.

Flasks: Clear glass that comes in two basic shapes, Florence and Erlenmeyer. They are measured in milliliters. A 250 milliliter is about five inches high and short of three inches wide at the bottom, narrowing to an inch and a half at the top.

Graduated Cylinders: Clear glass cylinders marked with measuring numbers and usually employed by lab technicians to accurately measure liquids; they are marked in milliliters. Cylinders are also available without the measuring lines etched in the glass and are called, naturally, ungraduated cylinders.

Museum Jars: Tall cylinders of glass made for display or the storage of specimens. They are measured in inches; a typical size is one foot high and two inches in diameter.

Show Bottles: Round-bottomed bottles with pinched-in necks, topped with a cork. They are usually filled with mineral specimens and stand on their corks. Remove the cork, tie nylon fishing line around the neck, and they make great hanging jars.

Volumetric Flasks: These have a round bottom, with just enough flat area to stand properly, and a very tall neck. They're measured in milliliters and serve as great-looking bud vases.

Test Tubes and Racks: Test-tube racks are still—sometimes—made of wood and hold six or twelve tubes. Put ivy cuttings in each one of the various test tubes, and you will have a fine display.

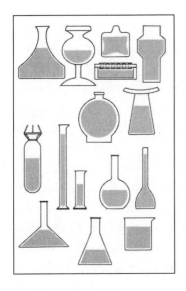
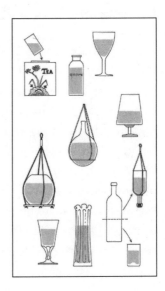

∧ Various chemical flasks and bottles.

BOTTLE CUTTERS

In the past few years, a number of different varieties of home bottle cutters have been marketed. I have been pleasantly surprised to find that, when the directions are followed properly, these devices really work, and many wine bottles can be turned into colored glassware that is economic, pleasing to look at, and helpful by not being thrown out to clutter the environment. My mayonnaise bottles, pickle bottles, and the like work perfectly as containers once their screw tops are removed. Depending on your free time and the amount of epoxy in the house, structures can be made that will reach the ceiling. Speaking of wine bottles, take the raffia off of a Chianti bottle, and you will be surprised to see that some now have flat bottoms.

HANGING GARDENS

Some hardware and department stores carry do-it-yourself kits consisting of small acrylic squares, strung with nylon fishing line that will hold almost any shape of container up to twenty-five pounds in weight. Consider these for a hanging bottle garden with plants held at various heights in front of a window or as a room divider.

You can make your own quite easily and support even more weight by using nylon cord or a fishing line of heavier test. Just drill a small hole in each corner of a piece of acrylic or plywood for a base. Then cut two pieces of cord the same length. Pass each cord through two of the holes (diagonally if you care to), and gather the ends. Slip a glass or plastic bead on the cords for tension, and tie them to a café-curtain ring. Vary the length of the cords, and you vary the heights of the bottles.

VASES

The number of flower holders based on clever design principles has rapidly increased. This past year, I've seen glass balls that hold flowers (or plants) combined with candles; bud vases made with twenty to thirty hollow glass rods bound together in cylindrical form; clear glass marbles wrapped in nylon fishnet for plant-holding frogs*; bent-glass tubing in many shapes and sizes; clear and colored acrylic flower pots; and still more variations on the old stand-bys. Many of them are perfect for a water garden.

And don't forget old cast-off containers. Use a small glass as a waterproof liner inside a tin tea canister. Concrete drain pipes and tiles can be stood on end and lined with a plastic or glass bottle to fill a corner with cascades of green. An old kerosene-lamp base, properly washed and filled with a few trailing plants, takes on a new look. Old bottling jars, electrical insulators, glasses from the supermarket, and even the old glass brick originally from the era of the thirties start life anew when used with plants.

*Round glass holders much like paperweights that have holes to insert stems of flowers.

6

Propagation Methods

ROOTED CUTTINGS

Have you ever wondered how the nursery industry gets all those plants? Well, much is achieved using rooted cuttings. When I want just a few plants, I've found the best method is a combination of small plastic pots full of sphagnum moss or wetted peat moss and a plastic baggie.

Find a healthy plant shoot on the mother plant. Then, using a clean, sharp knife or razor, cut it off slightly below the point where a leaf joins the stem. Remove any damaged leaves.

Make a hole in the growing medium with a pencil or similar object, then insert the cut shoot into the hole. Make sure the bottom of the stem touches the medium; that touch stimulus is what leads to new roots. Then, put the container with the new cutting into a plastic bag. Be sure to keep the growing medium moist. In a few weeks the leaf stem will grow roots, then you can move the plant to a water setup.

Another old-time method is rooting cuttings in a glass or jar of plain water. This works for ivies, impatiens, coleus, begonias, wandering inch plants, geraniums, and many more. You will be amazed at how fast these roots will grow, and you will soon have an army of plants to grow on in containers of water and pebbles.

OFFSHOOTS

Most bromeliads will bloom only once; the mother plant will die within a few months after flowering. But before she passes from the scene, new little plants, called offshoots, will grow around the base of the plant.

When these offshoots reach a height of six or eight inches, cut them off with a sharp knife. Take the offshoots and plant them in a weathered log or piece of wood, where your present epiphytes are now ensconced. Simply drill three-quarter-inch-diameter holes into the wood, pack the holes with sphagnum moss, then insert the offshoots.

LEAF CUTTINGS

There is a limit to the number of new plants that can be produced by rooted cuttings; the mother plant has a finite number of suitable stems. But if you're in no great rush and wish to reproduce a number of a particular plant, then leaf cuttings are the answer.

With large begonias, such as a Begonia rex, choose a large and healthy leaf with just a short stem and turn it upside down so the veins on the leaf bottom clearly show. Then, cut the main veins with a sharp knife, like a utility knife blade, at the vein junctions. Then lay the leaf on a moist bed of sand or peat moss, underside down, and cover with a baggie greenhouse.

Soon new little plantlets will appear. Once they grow to a few inches in size, they can be moved on to damp mix and eventually into a pot of water and pebbles.

CANE SECTIONING

Dracaenas, dieffenbachias, and cordylines are easily propagated by cutting stems into three-inch sections, making sure each section includes a leaf scar. Place the stems horizontally on a bed of moist sphagnum or peat moss and cover with a baggie greenhouse. When rooting is well along, the dormant bud will sprout and a new plant is on the way.

PLANTS BY DIVISION

Another easy way of producing new plants is by division of the root stock. Early spring is the best time, before new growth for the season begins. This process works with plants that form multiple crowns. The plant can be divided into as many new plants are there are crowns to work with.

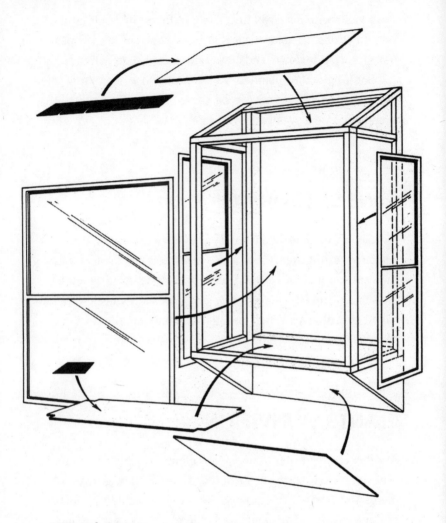

Materials List:

- Four white aluminum storm windows
- ¾-inch AA plywood (exterior grade)
- Standard two-by-fours
- Standard one-by-twos
- Roof shingling
- Screws

7

DIY Greenhouse Windows

LARGE WINDOW GARDEN

A greenhouse window like the one illustrated can be made from aluminum storm windows purchased at a local lumber-yard. The greenhouse window I built was designed to fit an opening in the outer wall of the front room that originally held a large wooden-framed window.

The roof of my new greenhouse was shingled instead of using glass, because the winter sun is so low in the sky I knew I could do without the extra light. The constructed greenhouse projected eighteen inches out from the side of the house, so I used two narrow aluminum storm windows to create the sides of the greenhouse. The floor of the greenhouse was constructed of marine plywood, which I covered with black vinyl slate. Two sheets of acrylic in wooden frames were hinged to the inside of the old window frame and closed the greenhouse to the room during the worst of the winter. Finally, an electrician installed an outlet under the window, so I can use a small electric heater to keep the plants warm on very cold days.

The screens that come with aluminum storm windows provide adequate ventilation in the summer and also help cut summer sunlight for sensitive plants.

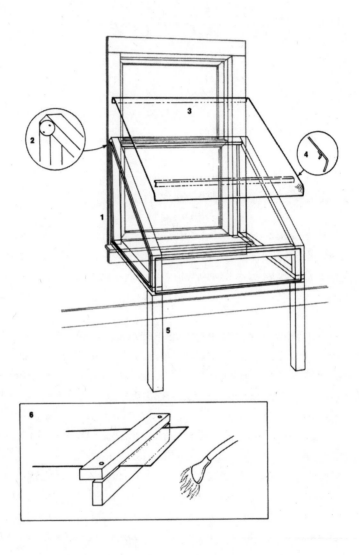

SMALL ACRYLIC WINDOW GARDEN

1. The basic frame is made of one-by-twos. Use a sliding T-square to figure the side frame angles. Measure and cut the pieces, and then, screw the frame together. The plywood bottom will rest on the windowsill. Measure and cut the plywood bottom to size; this piece will rest on the windowsill.

2. Measure and cut the acrylic side panels to size. Then, attach to the frame with screws. Cut two cross pieces from the one-by-twos and attach to the frame with 1 ½-inch No. 8 sheet metal screws. Then, use screws to attach the frame to the plywood bottom. Next, attach the front piece of acrylic to the frame and the front edge of the plywood bottom with screws.

3. The top cover piece of acrylic will need to be bent to fit with the application of heat (see step 6). This forms a good seal and adds rigidity to the plastic.

4. A small plastic strip is glued to the bottom of the cover to catch condensation so it will drip into the unit instead of on the floor.

5. The leg supports are constructed of two-by-threes. Use screws or hinges to attach the legs to the frame.

6. Use two one-by-twos attached with 6d nails hold the plastic sheet in place. Use a propane torch to heat the plastic; 300 degrees Fahrenheit is enough to soften this acrylic, so be careful to not get the flame too close. If the wood starts to char, you are too close! Move the torch back and forth across the acrylic where it leaves the wooden frame. When the plastic starts to drop down, press it with a dry rag or piece of wood. Once the desired angle is reached, rub the crease with a wet paper towel

to cool it. If you don't hold the sheet down as it cools, it will revert to its original shape. File and sand any sharp edges until they're smooth.

Materials List:
- Standard one-by-twos
- Standard two-by-threes
- 3/4-inch AA plywood (exterior grade)
- Acrylic panels
- Plastic strip
- Propane torch
- Wood screws
- 1 ½-inch No. 8 sheet metal screws
- 6d nails

Glossary

Bottle brushes: These bristle brushes are specially made for cleaning chemical glassware, including glass cylinders and various sizes of test tubes.

Bromeliads: Members of the great pineapple family, they have small, wiry roots that act as holdfasts so the plants that produce them cling to the bark of trees. Many of these plants are found in tropical areas of the world

Bulbs, including corms, pips, and pits: These replace the root systems for many plants. The most common bulb is the onion, but a large number of other plants grow from bulbs, crocuses from corms, lily-of-the-valley from pips, and plants like avocados from large seeds called pits.

Charcoal: Usually available as an aquarium supply item, it is used to absorb gases from decaying vegetation and to neutralize odors.

Clay pellets: Pellets made from clay that are used in various water gardens to allow roots to grow and anchor their attached plants in place.

Dust: Common dust accumulation on a plant's leaves will reduce the amount of light the plant needs; occasionally cleaning plants will help them thrive.

Epiphyte: A plant that grows above the ground on another plant, such as a tree, without negatively affecting the host plant. For example, bromeliads and orchids.

Foot candles: Used to measure the intensity of light. One foot candle (FC) is the amount of light cast on a white surface by one candle, one foot away, in an otherwise dark room.

Hydroculture: The process of growing plants in water instead of soil. It is generally used as a descriptive word in much of the world except the United States.

Hydroponics: The most common name given to the process of growing plants in water in the United States.

Insecticidal soaps: Used to control various pests, these are often a low-toxicity option compared to other types of pesticides.

Light: An essential ingredient to the survival of plants. Next to water, when growing any houseplants indoors, light is the most important consideration. Light intensity is measured in foot candles (FC).

Mist sprayers: Very handy to use to water the leaves of many plants grown in water, especially tropical foliage, like that of philodendrons, and many ferns.

Resources

Most of the equipment required, including plants in many cases, can now be found at variety stores, many department stores, and even, occasionally, at big box stores. In addition, a number of reputable firms ship plants by mail and delivery services.

Plants and Supplies

1000 Bulbs
Garland, Texas
www.1000bulbs.com
With hydroponic systems, parts, and supplies, they have all that you need to create a complete hydroponic system.

BetterGrowHydro
Pasadena, California
www.bghydro.com
Good selection of hydroponics tools for indoor gardeners of all levels, from beginner to pro.

Brent and Becky's Bulbs
Gloucester, Virginia
www.brentandbeckysbulbs.com
Offers a vast selection of bulbs as well as plants.

Carolina Biological Supply Company
Burlington, North Carolina
www.carolina.com
Supplier of chemical glassware, seedling sets, and hydroponic fertilizer experiment kits.

Edelweiss Gardens
Canby, Oregon
www.edelweissperennials.com
A mail order nursery specializing in choice perennials.

Edmund Scientific Company
Tonawanda, New York
www.scientificsonline.com
Offers a variety of chemical-safe glassware

Endless Spring
Shaftsbury, Vermont
www.endlesspringhydro.com
Carries a full line of products to keep your indoor garden blooming year-round.

Fifth Season Hydroponics
Stores in Asheville, Carrboro, Greensboro, and Raleigh, North Carolina, and Charlottesville, Virginia
www.fifthseasongardening.com/hydroponics
Offers an amazing amount of hydroponic supplies with stores in five locations.

Glasshouse Works
Stewart, Ohio
www.glasshouseworks.com
Along with a large variety of houseplants and bulbs, they also offer a nutrition formula for hydroponics.

GYOstuff Hydroponic & Indoor Garden Shop
Cambridge, Massachusetts
www.gyostuff.com
Offers advice, classes, and a wide range of gardening tools for hydroponic and other gardeners.

Greenlife Garden Supply
Billerica, Massachusetts; Biddeford and York, Maine; and Manchester, New Hampshire
www.greenlifegardensupply.com
Provides hydroponics supplies, from containers to videos.

Indoor Plant Kingdom
Portland, Maine
www.indoorplantkingdom.com
Offers year-round indoor gardening and hydroponics supplies, all you need to sustain an indoor garden.

Kartuz Greenhouses
Vista, California
www.kartuz.com
Offers a selection of begonias and other plants.

Logee's Greenhouses
Danielson, Connecticut
www.logees.com
Along with plant food, they carry a huge variety of indoor and windowsill plants.

McClure & Zimmerman
Randolph, Wisconsin
www.mzbulb.com
Provides flower bulbs and plant supports.

New England Hydroponics
Southampton and Framingham, Massachusetts
www.nehydro.com
Serving customers from coast to coast with a full selection of hydroponics gardening supplies, systems, and equipment.

Planet Natural
Bozeman, Montana
www.planetnatural.com
Provides a large variety of hydroponic gardening equipment that's suitable for growing indoors.

Rootdown Hydroponics Indoor Garden Center
Medford, Massachusetts
www.rootdownhydro.com
A unique selection of products tailed to help your indoor garden grow to its full potential.

Sunrise Hydroponics
Shawnee, Oklahoma
www.sunrisehydroponics.com
Carries a large stock of all things hydroponic, from garden accessories to growing mediums to pots and plant supports.

Ward's Natural Science Establishment
Rochester, New York
www.wardsci.com
Provides glassware and other hydroponic systems.

Websites

www.gardenweb.com — A discussion forum that includes more than six thousand entries related to hydroponics.

www.hydroponics.net/learn — An online resource that includes articles on heat, grow lights, nutrients, and more.

www.insideurbangreen.org — "Modern methods for growing food, foliage or flowers for the millions of us who are not green thumbs."

www.rain.org/global-garden/hydroponics-history.html — The history of hydroponics.

www.hydro-culture.net/faqs.html — Houseplant Hydro-culture's frequently asked questions.

Index

Page numbers marked with an asterisk indicate illustrations.

About the Author

Peter Loewer is a well-known writer, illustrator, print-maker, and botanical artist, who, over the past forty years, has written and illustrated more than twenty-five books on natural history and gardening, in addition to four science-based books for children, including the award-winning book *The Moonflower*. His book, *The Wild Gardener*, was named one of the best 75 Great Gardening Books of the Twentieth Century by the American Horticultural Society. He also wrote and illustrated *Bringing the Outdoors In*, *Growing and Decorating with Grasses*, *Thoreau's Garden*, *Jefferson's Garden*, *The Evening Garden*, and *Solving Deer Problems*, which is now in its second edition. He's also a specialist in vitreography, or using glass plates for lithography.

For years, Mr. Loewer ran an art studio in Manhattan that dealt with scientific illustration for college textbooks and medical art for various professional books on medicine. In 1968, he was the recipient of the Max Beckmann Fellowship to the Brooklyn Museum and continues to be a well-known lecturer on topics dealing with gardening and natural history and botanical art. His botanical illustrations are in the permanent collection of the Hunt Institute for Botanical Documentation at Carnegie-Mellon in Pittsburgh.

Today he is still writing and researching books dealing with horticulture and studies hydroponics and growing plants from seed. He teaches art history, American and international cinema, and botanical drawing at Asheville-Buncombe Technical College in Asheville, North Carolina.

Notes

Plant Name:

Date Received:_____Source:_____

Nutrient Solution Notes:_____

_____

_____

Light Source Notes:_____

_____

Temperature Notes:_____

_____

Plant Name:

Date Received:_____Source:_____

Nutrient Solution Notes:_____

_____

_____

Light Source Notes:_____

_____

Temperature Notes:_____

_____

Plant Name:

Date Received:_____Source:_____

Nutrient Solution Notes:_____

_____

_____

Light Source Notes:_____

_____

Temperature Notes:_____

_____

Plant Name:

Date Received:_____Source:_____

Nutrient Solution Notes:_____

_____

_____

Light Source Notes:_____

_____

Temperature Notes:_____

_____

Plant Name:

Date Received:_____Source:_____

Nutrient Solution Notes:_____

_____

_____

Light Source Notes:_____

_____

Temperature Notes:_____

_____

Plant Name:

Date Received:_____Source:_____

Nutrient Solution Notes:_____

_____

_____

Light Source Notes:_____

_____

Temperature Notes:_____

_____

Plant Name:

Date Received:_____Source:_____

Nutrient Solution Notes:_____

_____

_____

Light Source Notes:_____

_____

Temperature Notes:_____

_____

Plant Name:

Date Received:_____Source:_____

Nutrient Solution Notes:_____

_____

_____

Light Source Notes:_____

_____

Temperature Notes:_____

_____

Plant Name:

Date Received:_____Source:_____

Nutrient Solution Notes:_____

_____

_____

Light Source Notes:_____

_____

Temperature Notes:_____

_____

Plant Name:

Date Received:_____Source:_____

Nutrient Solution Notes:_____

_____

_____

Light Source Notes:_____

_____

Temperature Notes:_____

_____

Plant Name:

Date Received:_____Source:_____

Nutrient Solution Notes:_____

_____

_____

Light Source Notes:_____

_____

Temperature Notes:_____

_____

Plant Name:

Date Received:_____Source:_____

Nutrient Solution Notes:_____

_____

_____

Light Source Notes:_____

_____

Temperature Notes:_____

_____

Plant Name:

Date Received:_____Source:_____

Nutrient Solution Notes:_____

_____

_____

Light Source Notes:_____

_____

Temperature Notes:_____

_____

Plant Name:

Date Received:_____Source:_____

Nutrient Solution Notes:_____

_____

_____

Light Source Notes:_____

_____

Temperature Notes:_____

_____

Plant Name:

Date Received:_____Source:_____

Nutrient Solution Notes:_____

_____

_____

Light Source Notes:_____

_____

Temperature Notes:_____

_____

Plant Name:

Date Received:_____Source:_____

Nutrient Solution Notes:_____

_____

_____

Light Source Notes:_____

_____

Temperature Notes:_____

_____